First World War
and Army of Occupation
War Diary
France, Belgium and Germany

59 DIVISION
176 Infantry Brigade
Prince of Wales's (North Staffordshire Regiment)
2/5th Battalion
24 February 1917 - 31 January 1918

WO95/3021/3

The Naval & Military Press Ltd
www.nmarchive.com
Published in association with The National Archives

Published by

The Naval & Military Press Ltd

Unit 10 Ridgewood Industrial Park,

Uckfield, East Sussex,

TN22 5QE England

Tel: +44 (0) 1825 749494

www.naval-military-press.com

www.nmarchive.com

This diary has been reprinted in facsimile from the original. Any imperfections are inevitably reproduced and the quality may fall short of modern type and cartographic standards.

© **Crown Copyright**
Images reproduced by permission of The National Archives, London, England, 2015.

Contents

Document type	Place/Title	Date From	Date To
Heading	WO95/3021/3		
Heading	59th Division 176th Infy Bde 2-5th Bn Nth Staffs Regt 1917 Feb-1918 Jan And 1916 Jan & Feb		
War Diary	Godford	24/02/1917	24/02/1917
War Diary	Boulogne	25/02/1917	25/02/1917
War Diary	Salouel	26/02/1917	26/02/1917
War Diary	Fouilloy	27/02/1917	27/02/1917
War Diary	Morcourt	28/02/1917	04/03/1917
Heading	War Diary of 2/5th North Staffs Regt From 1st March 1917 To 31st March 1917 Vol II		
War Diary	Morcourt	01/03/1917	05/03/1917
War Diary	Foucaucourt	06/03/1917	06/03/1917
War Diary	Genermont	07/03/1917	11/03/1917
War Diary	Foucaucourt	12/03/1917	14/03/1917
War Diary	Genermont	15/03/1917	18/03/1917
War Diary	Mazencourt	19/03/1917	27/03/1917
War Diary	Brie	28/03/1917	31/03/1917
Heading	War Diary of 2/5th North Staffs Regiment From 1st April 1917 To 30th April 1917 Vol 3		
War Diary	Brie	01/04/1917	02/04/1917
War Diary	Estees-En-Chaussee	03/04/1917	03/04/1917
War Diary	Vraignes	04/04/1917	05/04/1917
War Diary	Hervilly	06/04/1917	10/04/1917
War Diary	Vendelles	11/04/1917	17/04/1917
War Diary	Le Verguier	18/04/1917	22/04/1917
War Diary	Jeancourt	23/04/1917	27/04/1917
War Diary	Le Verguier	28/04/1917	28/04/1917
War Diary	Hancourt	29/04/1917	30/04/1917
Heading	War Diary of 2/5th North Stafford Regiment From 1st May 1917 To 31st May 1917 Vol 4		
War Diary	Hancourt	01/05/1917	06/05/1917
War Diary	Villeret	08/05/1917	11/05/1917
War Diary	Hervilly	12/05/1917	15/05/1917
War Diary	Villeret	16/05/1917	20/05/1917
War Diary	Hervilly	21/05/1917	23/05/1917
War Diary	Templeux	24/05/1917	30/05/1917
War Diary	Hamelet	31/05/1917	31/05/1917
Heading	War Diary of 2/5th North Stafford Regiment From 1st June 1917 To 30th June 1917 Vol 5		
War Diary	Equancourt	01/06/1917	11/06/1917
War Diary	Beaucamp	12/06/1917	22/06/1917
War Diary	Metz	23/06/1917	30/06/1917
Heading	War Diary of 2/5th North Stafford Regiment From July 1st 1917 To July 31st 1917 Vol 6		
War Diary	Metz	01/07/1917	01/07/1917
War Diary	Equancourt	02/07/1917	07/07/1917
War Diary	Barastre	08/07/1917	31/07/1917
Heading	War Diary of 2/5th Bn North Staffordshire Regiment From 1st August 1917 To 31st August 1917 Vol 7		
War Diary	Barastre	01/08/1917	23/08/1917

War Diary	Forceville	23/08/1917	31/08/1917
Heading	War Diary of 2/5th Bn North Stafford Regiment From Sept 1st 1917 To Sept 30th 1917 Vol 8		
War Diary	Winnizeele	01/09/1917	18/09/1917
War Diary	Brandhoek	19/09/1917	20/09/1917
War Diary	Ypres North	21/09/1917	23/09/1917
War Diary	East of Wieltje	24/09/1917	24/09/1917
War Diary	Ypres	25/09/1917	25/09/1917
War Diary	East of Wieltje	26/09/1917	28/09/1917
War Diary	Vlamertinghe	29/09/1917	29/09/1917
War Diary	Watou	30/09/1917	30/09/1917
Operation(al) Order(s)	Battalion Operation Orders No.42 By Lieut-Col. H. Johnson Commanding 2/5th Bn North Stafford Regiment	21/09/1917	21/09/1917
Operation(al) Order(s)	Battalion Operation Orders No.43 By Lieut-Col. H. Johnson Commanding 2/5th Bn North Stafford Regiment	21/09/1917	21/09/1917
Operation(al) Order(s)	Battalion Operation Orders No.44 By Lieut-Col. H. Johnson Commanding 2/5th Bn North Stafford Regiment	23/09/1917	23/09/1917
Miscellaneous	Amendments to Bn. Operation Order No.44		
Operation(al) Order(s)	Battalion Operation Orders No.47, By Lieut-Col. H. Johnson Commanding 2/5th Bn. North Stafford Regiment	25/09/1917	25/09/1917
Heading	War Diary of 2/5th North Staffs Regiment From 1st Oct 1917 To 31st Oct 1917 Vol 9		
War Diary	Watou	01/10/1917	01/10/1917
War Diary	Guarbecque	02/10/1917	07/10/1917
War Diary	Crepy	08/10/1917	10/10/1917
War Diary	Sains-En-Gohelle	11/10/1917	12/10/1917
War Diary	Noulette Huts	13/10/1917	13/10/1917
War Diary	Lievin and Lens	14/10/1917	21/10/1917
War Diary	Lievin	22/10/1917	29/10/1917
War Diary	Gouy-Servins	30/10/1917	31/10/1917
Heading	War Diary of 2/5th North Staffs Regiment From 1st Nov 1917 To 30th Nov 1917 Vol 10		
War Diary	Gouy-Servins	01/11/1917	06/11/1917
War Diary	La Covlotte	07/11/1917	13/11/1917
War Diary	Red Trench	14/11/1917	16/11/1917
War Diary	Souchez Camp	17/11/1917	17/11/1917
War Diary	Gouy Servins	18/11/1917	18/11/1917
War Diary	Petit Servins	19/11/1917	19/11/1917
War Diary	Bernville	20/11/1917	21/11/1917
War Diary	Courcelles	22/11/1917	22/11/1917
War Diary	Le Comte	23/11/1917	23/11/1917
War Diary	Heudicourt	24/11/1917	27/11/1917
War Diary	Ribecourt	28/11/1917	28/11/1917
War Diary	South Of Bourlon Wood	29/11/1917	30/11/1917
Heading	War Diary of 2/5th North Staffs Regiment From 1st Dec 1917 To 31st Dec 1917 Vol 11		
War Diary	South Of Bourlon Wood	01/12/1917	02/12/1917
War Diary	Flesquieres	03/12/1917	05/12/1917
War Diary	Pioneer Camp	06/12/1917	10/12/1917
War Diary	Hindenburg Support	11/12/1917	13/12/1917
War Diary	Flesquieres	14/12/1917	18/12/1917
War Diary	Trescault	19/12/1917	20/12/1917

War Diary	Barastre	21/12/1917	25/12/1917
War Diary	Liencourt	26/12/1917	31/12/1917
Heading	War Diary of 2/5th Bn North Staffs Regiment From 1st Jan 1918 To 31st Jan 1918 Vol 12		
War Diary	Liencourt	01/01/1918	31/01/1918

Woods 3021/3

59TH DIVISION
176TH INFY BDE

2-5TH BN NTH STAFFS REGT
1917 FEB – DEC 1917 1918 JAN
AND 1918 JAN & FEB

Absorbed by 5 BN FEB 1918

…

WAR DIARY

INTELLIGENCE SUMMARY

Army Form C. 2118

Vol I

2/5 Batt: North Staff Regt.

VOLUME No II.

Instructions regarding War Diaries and Intelligence Summaries are contained in F.S. Regs, Part II. and the Staff Manual respectively. Title Pages will be prepared in manuscript.

(Erase heading not required.)

Place	Date	Hour	Summary of Events and Information	Remarks and references to Appendices
England.	24.2.17	8.30pm (11.30pm)	The Battalion entrains for Folkestone, 20 Officers, 802 other ranks. Names of Officers as follows:— Lt.Col: Sir A. Bomoymorz. Bart. Major O.C. Bladen. Capt: J. Hodgkinson. " C. Potley (from 4(Res) N/Sf. Regt.) " T.E. Taberts. " W.N. Blathn. " E.B.H. Soame. " F.D. Bennett. " N.H. Lass (R.A.M.C.) T. Lieut. Colly. V.B. Shelley Lieut: L.E. Bullock " L.H. Ormrode 2nd " J.G.H. Magnu " F.J. Cook " R.M. Trimble " L.M. Pollard " E. Carhart " A. Peach 2 Lieut: R.B.C. Abel attached Capt: Heap. R.C. Chaplain	V.B.S.
Boulogne.	25.2.17	3.0AM 5.30AM 9.30AM 2.10PM	Arrive Folkestone & proceed to Rest Camp. Embark on Troopship. Disembark at Boulogne & proceed to OSTROHOVE Rest Camp.	V.B.S.
Saleux.	26.2.17	8.30AM 4.10PM	Entrain at Boulogne station. Arrive at SALEUX station & march to SALEUEL where the Battalion is billeted.	V.B.S.
Fouilloy.	27.2.17	8.30AM 5.30PM	Leave SALEUEL & march to FOUILLOY, 17 miles via LONGUEAU where we are joined by the Transport Party consisting of 3 Officers:— Major H. Johnson, Lieut. D.A. Smith & 2Lt D. Alexander, and 87 other ranks, Transport consists of:— + also Lt. T. Sidlow & 30th ranks, Horses. 12 Riding 35 Draught 7 Pack. Vehicles. 10 Limbers. 4 Field Kitchens. 2 Water Carts. 1 Maltese Cart 1 Officers Mess Cart. Arrive at FOUILLOY where the Battalion is billeted.	C.B.S.

Army Form C. 2118

WAR DIARY
or
INTELLIGENCE SUMMARY
(Erase heading not required.)

2/5" Batt: North Staff Regt.

Place	Date	Hour	Summary of Events and Information	Remarks and references to Appendices
Morcourt	28.2.17	8:30 PM	Leave FOUILLOY & march to MORCOURT about 10 miles.	108
— "	1.3.17	3:0 PM	Arrive in MORCOURT & proceed to No 54 Camp, Hutments. Nil.	108
— "	2.3.17	7:0 PM	4 Officers, 11 other ranks. (Lieut L.H. Jones sick in hospital) 2nd Lieut W. Proctor, 2nd Lieut R.B. Bloore, 2nd Lieut A.R. Catton, who proceeded to France on Feb 2nd as an Advanced Party & attached to 8th D.L.I. for instruction return to the Battalion.	105
— "	3.3.17	2.0 PM	7 Officers and 3 Platoons, one each from A.B. + C Coys proceed to FOUCAUCOURT to be attached to the 9th D.L.I, 151st Inf. Bde for instruction.	108
— "	4.3.17	2.0 PM	1 Officer and one Platoon proceed to FOUCAUCOURT to be attached to the Reserve Coy of the 9th D.L.I.	108

M Bannerman Lt Col
2/5 N Staffs.

Original

Army Form C. 2118.

WAR DIARY
or
INTELLIGENCE SUMMARY.
(Erase heading not required.)

Instructions regarding War Diaries and Intelligence Summaries are contained in F. S. Regs., Part II. and the Staff Manual respectively. Title pages will be prepared in manuscript.

Hour, Date, Place	Summary of Events and Information	Remarks and references to Appendices
	Confidential War Diary of 2/5TH North Staffs Regt. From 1st March 1917 To 31st March 1917	Vol II 59th Div.

WAR DIARY or INTELLIGENCE SUMMARY

Army Form C. 2118

Volume II. March 1917

2/5" Batt. D. Staff Regt.

Page 3

Place	Date	Hour	Summary of Events and Information	Remarks and references to Appendices
Morcourt	3/1/17	—	Nil. Strength 27 Officers. 926 other ranks.	
"	2 "	9.0 am	4 Officers 11 O.R.S (incl. 2nd Lieut. D.H. Jones sick in hospital) 2nd Lieut P.B. Blair, 2nd Lieut A.R. Cotton who proceeded to France on Feb 2nd as an Advanced Party & were attached to the 8" D.C.I. for instruction returned to the Battalion.	WB
"	3 "	2.0 pm	7 Officers and 3 Platoons, one each from A, B, C Coys proceeded to FOUCAUCOURT to be attached to the 9" D.L.I. 151st Inf. Bde for instructions.	WB
"	4 "	2.0 pm	1 Officer and 1 Platoon proceed to FOUCAUCOURT to be attached to the Support Company of the 9" D.L.I. for instructions.	WB
"	5 "	9.0 am	The Battalion marches away on route for FOUCAUCOURT about 10 miles.	WB
		2.0 pm	Arrive in FOUCAUCOURT. The men are billeted in H. Loggs Huts. The Officers in small Huts and dugouts	
FOUCAUCOURT	6 "	5.0 pm	The Battalion less the 4 Platoons already in the trenches moved off from FOUCAUCOURT to relieve the 9" D.L.I. in the trenches, route via. ESTREES and BERNY, which was not complete till midnight owing to the muddy condition of the ground, in many places the trenches were impassable. The trenches taken over were situated round the village of GENERMONT (T.9.c. Central) now completely demolished. The right flank of the line was at T.H.b.7.4. and the left flank at T.9.d.32. Battalion H.Q.s being at T.9.c.2.9. The Front line Red Red Hat close to Skypt. "D" Company R.B.s "C" at T.9.c.4.5. Left Coy "B" at T.9.c.9.9. and Support Coy "D" in GRENADIERS TRENCH at T.9.b.64. The front line extended about 1100 yds and was not held except by Sentry Groups, in front of the trenches were right posts placed in trenches running from 100 to 200 yds in front of the line, in some of these were Lewis Guns. The trenches, especially the front line were in a very muddy condition, the population in many places the Collapsed leaving the trenches any depth to many fire & walk has to be taken as care in clearing up & repairing them. 1 M. G. wounded. (Self-inflicted)	WB

Army Form C. 2118

WAR DIARY
or
INTELLIGENCE SUMMARY
(Erase heading not required.)

Volume No I March 1917

2/5th Batt. North Stafford Regt

Instructions regarding War Diaries and Intelligence Summaries are contained in F. S. Regs., Part II. and the Staff Manual respectively. Title Pages will be prepared in manuscript.

Place	Date	Hour	Summary of Events and Information	Remarks and references to Appendices
Cont.	6 3/17	...	Study of Water. The Bn. to be cleaned up owing of heated terms & carrying parties fetching all the water from BERNY about 1400 yds behind head quarters. Rations. These could only be brought up at night & as timber could not get any closer than BERNY the rations, had all to were made at into dumbogal & carried up on the track house & other parties went for the horses, these parties were brought up to about T.8.6.9.2, a point about 200yds from Battalion Headquarters.	188
GENERMONT	7 "	...	Ground still in a very muddy state, very little activity on front of the enemy.	188
— "	8 "	4·10am	1. Man wounded (self-inflicted.)	188
— "	9 "	9·0pm	1. Man wounded (self-inflicted.)	188
— "	10 "	8·0pm	Relief by 2/6" S. Staffs Regt commenced, owing to the muddy condition of the ground relief not complete till 10 AM on the 11th	188
— "	11 "	5·0am	Arrive back at FOUCAUCOURT and proceed to POMMIERES CAMP, R26.C.8.5, the support company having completed its relief first had arrived at 2·30 am	188
FOUCAUCOURT	12 "	...	Remain in Brigade Reserve.	188
— "	13 "	...	d.ito	188
— "	14 "	6·0pm	The Battalion moved off from FOUCAUCOURT to relieve the 2/6" S. Staffs Regt in the trenches previously held, great difficulties experienced in the relief owing to the muddy state of the ground & relief was not complete till 3·0 AM on the 15th	188
GENERMONT	15 "	...	Nil	188
— "	16 "	...	Casualties, 1. Killed by bullet wound in stomach from sniper, 9 wounded, 1 bullet wound in face from a sniper, 2 shrapnel wounds from a German rifle grenade.	188

1875 Wt. W593/826 1,000,000 4/15 J.B.C. & A. A.D.S.S./Forms/C. 2118.

Army Form C. 2118

WAR DIARY
or
INTELLIGENCE SUMMARY

(Erase heading not required.)

Volume No. 2 March 1917   2/5" Batt: North Stafford Regt
Page 5

Place	Date	Hour	Summary of Events and Information	Remarks and references to Appendices
GENERMONT	17 3/17	1.0 a.m.	Heavy artillery bombardment on the German position commenced by our guns lasting till 4.0 a.m. in conjunction with the French who were preparing to attack on the south, south of ROYE.	A.98
		9.0 a.m.	Message received from Bde H.Qrs. that the enemy had evacuated his trenches & patrols are sent out to verify this and report all clear & no enemy in sight	
		6.0 p.m.	Outpost line formed along the LILLE Rd. from junction of LILLE Rd. and railway T.16.d.9.8. on the right to a point T.11.c.2.6. on the same road, two companies find the outpost, "D" on the right and "C" on the left. The chaining line being the south end of MAZENCOURT T.16.b.8.6.	
"	18 "	1.0 p.m.	Patrols report that the country in front EAST of the RIVER SOMME is clear of the enemy & that no sign of the enemy can be seen on the WEST side of the river.	
"	"	4.0 a.m.	Battalion Headquarters moves forward and occupies a Quarry at T.17.a.0.5; the remainder of B, C & D Companies move forward & find billets in MAZENCOURT, "D" Company remaining behind in the old outpost trenches to act as a carrying party for water and rations	
"	"	6.0 a.m.	A Patrol from "C" & "D" Companies moves forward & occupies DAME BLANCHE and POULE VERTE Trenches from T.2.H. & 9.2. on the right to T.18.c.2.8. on the left, touch being obtained on the right with the 2/6" WARWICKSHIRE REGT, 182 Bde and on the 2/4 with the 2/6 " N. STAFFORD REGT, the line of advance being the VILLIERS-CARBONNEL —— MAZENCOURT Rd.	A.98
MAZENCOURT	19 "		Observation Patrols are pushed overlooking the RIVER SOMME but no trace of the enemy is seen	A.98
"	20 "	9.0 a.m.	"A" Company which had been left behind comes up & billets in MISERY. Patrols found by "C" + "D" Coys occupying the DAME BLANCHE and POULE VERTE TRENCHES are relieved by "F" Company, work commenced clearing the day in converting these trenches to face EASTWARDS	A.98

Army Form C. 2118

WAR DIARY
or
INTELLIGENCE SUMMARY

2/5" Batt. North Stafford Regt.

(Erase heading not required.)

Volume II March 1917

Instructions regarding War Diaries and Intelligence Summaries are contained in F.S. Regs., Part II. and the Staff Manual respectively. Title Pages will be prepared in manuscript.

Page 6.

Place	Date	Hour	Summary of Events and Information	Remarks and references to Appendices
MAZENCOURT	21st	.....	Work continued on the DAME BLANCHE and POULE VERTE TRENCHES.	138
"	22 "	.....	2/Lieut Kawford arrived & proceeded to MISERY, the details and Battalion Quartermaster Stores remaining at BERRY	138
"	23 "	.....	Details and Battalion Quartermaster Stores arrive and are accommodated in MISERY.	138
"	24 "	.....	Nil	
"	25 "	.....	The 59th Division takes over part of the 48th Divisional Front & the 61st Division part of the 59th Divisional Front the 2/5"B. Staff Regt. Part of the 2/6"B. Staff Regt. the new line being along the line POULE VERTE VICTRICE TRENCHES from T18 C.87 on the right to the Southern end of HORSE CORSE inclusive, this line is still held by a Batt. and for defense is divided up as follows:— "B" Confong from T18 C.87 — T18 B.28 "C" " — " — T18 B.28 — T12 d.81 "D" " — " — T12 d.81 — Southern edge of HORSE CORSE inclusive. "H" — " — Withdrawing its field to MISERY to form a Support	138
"	26 "	.....	Strength the following officers having arrived from the 3rd (Reserve) N. Staff Regt. on the date mentioned are taken on the strength accordingly:— 2nd Lieut J.G. Brettle. 17-3-17. " " L.C. Salt. 20-3-17. 2nd Lieut P.G. Cave being posted for duty with 176th Light Trench Mortar Battery is struck off the strength Pvt. Lieut. C.O.B. Brokelsbank 21-3-17 " — W/Pot Brown. 21-3-17. 2nd Lt. Pidler returned to unit is taken on the strength.	139 138
"	27 "	10·15 am	Battalion leaves MAZENCOURT on route for BRIE Via VILLERS-CARBONNEL and good into Divisional Reserve while taking over that portion of the defences of BRIE Bridge-Head North of the BRIE-MONS-EN-CHAUSSEE road, the defences on our right flank and South of the above road being held by the 2/5" South Stafford Regt P.T.O.	138

WAR DIARY or INTELLIGENCE SUMMARY

Army Form C. 2118

Volume No II. March 1917.

2/5 Batt. North Stafford Regt.

Place	Date	Hour	Summary of Events and Information	Remarks and references to Appendices
contd	27/3/17	3-0 P.M.	Arrive at BRIE at 3-0 P.M. the Trenches allotted as follows- the front line being BINGEN Trench from O29 d 34 on the right to O22 d 35 thence by a new trench partly dug to O22 a.00, the support line being NASSAU Trench:- "D" Company in the front line trench from O29 d 34 to O23 C 50, "C" Company in the front line trench from O23 C 50 to O22 d 35, "B" Company the new trench from O22 d 35 to O22 a.00 and "A" Company in support in NASSAU Trench	WD
BRIE	28 3/17		Work commenced on the Trenches, taking down German wire entanglements and replacing on the West side of the front line trench, digging new trench from O22 d 35 — O22 a.00.	WD
—"—	29 3/17		— ditto —	WD
—"—	30 "		Batt: Quartermaster Stores which remained at MISERY Commenced to move up to MONS-EN-CHAUSSEE.	WD
—"—	31 "		Batt: Quartermaster Stores & Transport complete move to MONS-EN-CHAUSSEE, the battalion remaining at BRIE.	WD

In the Field
31-3-17

M Bannerman Lieut.Col.
Comdg 2/5 N. Staff Regt.

Army Form C. 2118.

WAR DIARY
or
INTELLIGENCE SUMMARY.
(Erase heading not required.)

Instructions regarding War Diaries and Intelligence Summaries are contained in F. S. Regs., Part II. and the Staff Manual respectively. Title pages will be prepared in manuscript.

Vol 3

Confidential

Original

War Diary

of

2/5th North Staffs Regiment

From — 1st April, 1917.
To — 30th April, 1917.

WAR DIARY or INTELLIGENCE SUMMARY

Army Form C. 2118

Volume II Oct. 1917

2/5th Batt: North Stafford Regt.

Place	Date	Hour	Summary of Events and Information	Remarks and references to Appendices
BRIE	1 4/17	....	Strength 30 Officers. 896 Other Ranks	US
"	2 --	9.0 am	Left BRIE and march to ESTREES-EN-CHAUSSEE.	US
		10.30 am	The Battalion arrived and is billeted in ESTREES-EN-CHAUSSEE. The Quartermasters Stores and transport remaining in MONS-EN-CHAUSSEE.	
		....	Strength. 1 officer reports from the 3rd North Stafford Regt who takes on the Strength. 2nd Lieut. G. GREVILLE	
ESTREES-EN-CHAUSSEE	3 --	9.0 am	Commence work on the defences EAST of VRAIGNES, digging of 5 overhead posts commenced.	US
		5.0 PM	Move to VRAIGNES commenced after short notice	
		7.0 PM	Those could't of the Battalion billetted in VRAIGNES.	
		...	Strength. 1 officer reports from the 3rd North Stafford Regt & is taken on the Strength, 2nd Lieut. N.H. MARSON.	
VRAIGNES	4 --	6.0 PM	Working party of 400 other ranks, 100 per company proceed to HERVILLY to dig posts which are taken over later.	US
" --	5 --	3.0 PM	The posts are taken over from the 2/4th Lincolns the remainder of the Battalion arriving in HERVILLY at 10.0 A.M., the Lewis Gun posts as follows:- 2 Coys being in the front line and 2 Coys in support at HERVILLY. Position of posts held by B and C Coys in front line were as follows:- "C" Right Coy. "B" Left Coy. Map reference 62c N.E.	US

	Right Coy				Left Coy			
No. of Ppl.	Map reference.	Garrison.	No. L. Guns.	No. of Ppl.	Map reference	Garrison.	No. L. Guns.
No. 1.	L. 19. d. 9. 7.	1 Platoon	1	No. 3	L. 15. c. 4.4.	1 Platoon	1
" 2	L. 20. a. 5. 2.	- do. -	1	Support	L. 14. c. 6. 6.	- do. -	1
Support	L. 19. d. 6. 8.	- do. -	2	Coy. H.Q.	L. 13. d. 7. 4.	- do. -	2
L. Gun Ppl	L. 19. d. 9. 0.		1		L. 13. d. 7. 4.		
Coy. H.Q.	L. 19. d. 9. 8.	1 N.C.O. 9 men.					

Army Form C. 2118

Volume II. April 1917

WAR DIARY
INTELLIGENCE SUMMARY

2/5 Bn. North Stafford Regt.

(Erase heading not required.)

Instructions regarding War Diaries and Intelligence Summaries are contained in F.S. Regs., Part II. and the Staff Manual respectively. Title Pages will be prepared in manuscript.

Place	Date	Hour	Summary of Events and Information	Remarks and references to Appendices
VRAIGNES.	5	7 p.m.	2 Companies in support go up into line to assist "B" and "C" Coys to improve their posts and commence wiring. CASUALTIES. – NIL.	A88
HERVILLY.	6	7 p.m.	"B" and "C" Coys in the front line are relieved by "A" and "D" Coys. "B" Coy returns to reed and "C" Coy remains during the night to assist in covering the posts. CASUALTIES. – NIL.	A88
– do –	7	7 p.m.	"B" Coy sends Wiring Party to assist "A" and "D" Coys in the line to wire and push forward their posts Nos. 1, 2 and 3. So that a full view of the enemy trenches between FERVAQUE FARM and LE VERGUIER could be obtained. STRENGTH. – The undermentioned 2 Officers report from the 3rd S.N. Staffs. Regt. and are taken on the strength. – 2/Lt. W. HAYWARD and 2/Lt. E.M. COPE. CASUALTIES. – NIL.	A88
– do –	8	7 p.m.	"A" and "D" Coys are relieved by "B" and "C" Coys. "D" Coy returning to reed, and "A" Coy remaining to assist "B" and "C" in the work commenced the previous night. At 9 p.m. orders received to cease work, so the men can rest to be ready to take part in an attack next day. CASUALTIES. – NIL.	A88
– do –	9	9 a.m.	After receiving a report that the Germans had evacuated the trenches south of LE VERGUIER a patrol was sent out to investigate. This patrol reported that it was fired on by at least 6 of the enemy. A further patrol of one officer and 3 O.R. was sent out and was fired on by M.G. fire and at last 12 rifles from the direction of FERVAQUE FARM.	
		12.45 p.m.	A Platoon under 2/Lt. W. HAYWARD left CAPEZA COPSE in order to rectify the German trench in front of GRAND PRIEL WOOD	A88
		1.45 p.m.	Though they were met with heavy M.G. and rifle fire from FERVAQUE FARM, they succeeded in rushing the wire, cutting a way through, and reoccupying the German trench. In doing this	

WAR DIARY
or
INTELLIGENCE SUMMARY
(Erase heading not required.)

Volume II April 1917.
Page 10. 2/5 Bn. North Stafford Regiment

Army Form C. 2118

Place	Date	Hour	Summary of Events and Information	Remarks and references to Appendices
HERVILLY.	9th		They sustained 5 casualties. This party was reinforced at once by one platoon of "C" Coy, with one Lewis Gun, and preparations were at once made for "D" Coy to move forward and occupy the new line. Patrols sent out by 2/6 N. Stafford into GRAND PRIEL WOODS caught sight of the retiring Germans, and fired on them, but without effect. Later, a patrol of "C" Coy on consolidating GRAND PRIEL WOODS encountered enemy snipers, and Serjt. Clews was shot through the heart. Consolidation was at once commenced, and steps taken to hold the old German line. CASUALTIES. — KILLED:— 1st N. Stafford Regt. 2 I.R. WOUNDED:— 6 other ranks.	W.D.
-do-	10th		The line being held by us was the old German trench from L.21.d.6.b.t. on the right to FERVAQUE FARM on the left, the 2/6 North Staffs. Regt. being on our right, and a Battalion of the 179 Bde. on our left. The above occupied an advance post at L.22.c.7.7. Orders were received from O.C. 2/6 NORTH STAFFS. REGT. (who had come up to HERVILLY the previous evening, and was now in command of the Bde. Left Sector) C Coy advanced their line, and occupied a position from L.22.6.W. to L.22.f.8.t. so as to gain touch with the troops of the 2/6 NORTH STAFFS REGT. which had, during the previous night, advanced through our line and dug itself in about 1400 yds in front of the German trench occupied by us. As the line now occupied by "C" Coy was under observation by the Germans they were heavily shelled during the afternoon, resulting in several casualties.	W.D.

WAR DIARY
INTELLIGENCE SUMMARY
(Erase heading not required.)

Army Form C. 2118

Volume II April. 1917
2/5 Bn. North Stafford Regt.

Place	Date	Hour	Summary of Events and Information	Remarks and references to Appendices
HERVILLY.	10	3.30 p.m.	As the above line held by "C" Coy was without shelter of any kind they were ordered to withdraw to the trench they had previously held.	
		11 p.m.	Orders were received that the Battalion was to be relieved by one Battalion from the rubble, and guides were sent to meet them at CAPEZA COPSE at 5 a.m. The relieving Battalion, however, did not arrive at this time, and "B" Coy, the final Coy to be relieved, did not complete its relief till 1 a.m. the following morning, marching at once to VENDELLES to occupy billets which had been arranged during the day. CASUALTIES. - KILLED:- 2/Lt. W.M.R. Pollard, and 3 O.R. WOUNDED:- 4 O.R.	48
VENDELLES	11	5 a.m.	"C" Coy, which had not yet been relieved, was relieved by "D" Coy, who had been in reserve in a quarry at L.13.d.7.5., and proceeded to VENDELLES.	
		6 p.m.	As the relief of "A" and "D" Coys still in the line was reported by the relieving Bn. of the 177 Bde. to be taking place, Bn. H.Q. moved to VENDELLES. These 2 Coys however, were not relieved until 1 a.m. next morning, and they did not arrive in VENDELLES until 5 a.m. CASUALTIES.- NIL.	48
-do.-	12		Remain in VENDELLES as Support Bn. to the Bde. right sub-sector, the 2/5 South Staffs. Regt. being in the front line. The following posts, east of VENDELLES, are being held by us. L.32.d.1.9. L.32.d.9.0. R.9.a.V.8. - The 2/6 North Staff. Regt. holding the afternoon posts on our left east of JEANCOURT are a Bn. of the 106 Bde on our right. - CASUALTIES. - NIL.	48

WAR DIARY / INTELLIGENCE SUMMARY

Army Form C. 2118

Volume II. April 1917

2/5 Bn. North Stafford Regt.

Place	Date	Hour	Summary of Events and Information	Remarks and references to Appendices
VENDELLES	13th	7pm	"D" Coy send a Working Party consisting of 2 Platoons to construct a road at K.6.a.3.b. in front of the line occupied by the 2/5 South Stafford Regt. and "A" Coy send a Carrying Party of 100 others ranks to carry up wiring material for this Battalion. CASUALTIES:- NIL.	
VENDELLES	14th	7pm	"B" and "C" Coys send working and carrying parties to avoid the 2/6 South Stafford Regt. on the front line of the Bde right subsector. CASUALTIES:- NIL.	
-do-	15th	7pm	"A" and "D" Coys send working and carrying parties to avoid 2/South Stafford Regt. CASUALTIES:- NIL.	
-do-	16th		Orders received in the morning to relieve 2/6 South Stafford Regt. during the night of 16/17 - holding the front line on the Bde Right Subsector, but at 3 p.m. these orders are cancelled and orders received for the Bn. to occupy a line from M.1.a.3.8. on the right along 120 contour to L.36.a.1.9 on left and to dig and establish posts along this line - which was in front of the line held by 2/5 Bn. South Stafford Regt.	
		8pm	Bn. leaves VENDELLES. "A" and "D" Coys to dig in and occupy the abovementioned line and "B" and "C" Coys are held in reserve to act as carrying Parties to carry forward ammunition and stores - but owing to the wet weather and the muddy state of	

Army Form C. 2118

WAR DIARY
or
INTELLIGENCE SUMMARY
(Erase heading not required.)

Volume II. April 1917.
Page 14.
2/5 Bn. North Stafford Regt.

Instructions regarding War Diaries and Intelligence Summaries are contained in F.S. Regs, Part II. and the Staff Manual respectively. Title Pages will be prepared in manuscript.

Place	Date	Hour	Summary of Events and Information	Remarks and references to Appendices
VENDELLES.	16th	8 p.m.	The roads, this was found to be impracticable in the time, and at dawn the disposition of the Bn. was as follows:- "B" Coy returned to buffalo at VENDELLES; "C" Coy to overflow road at L.32.c.9.9. - and "A" and "D" Coys remained for the day in the support line. CASUALTIES:- NIL.	ASS
—do—	17th	7.30 p.m.	"B" and "C" Coys move up and commence to dig posts along the line previously mentioned which at dawn are occupied by 2 platoons of "D" Coy with one platoon in support at R.S.d.8.8. - "B" and "C" Coys returning to the posts occupied by them by previous night, and "A" Coy - who had been acting as a carrying party during the night, remain in the neighbourhood trenches of the 2/5 South Stafford Regt. CASUALTIES:- NIL.	ASS
LE VERGUIER.	18th	7.30 p.m.	"B" Coy move forward and relieve "D" Coy occupying the posts in the front line, and after relief "D" Coy occupy the posts in the front line, and carry on digging and improving the posts commenced the previous night. "C" Coy move forward and erect shelters along the hedge at L.34.a.3.6. "A" Coy acting as carrying party. Bn. H.Q. move forward to L.34.d.3.6. CASUALTIES:- Wounded in action - 4 O.R.	NSP
—do—	19th		Disposition of the Bn. on the morning of 19th is as follows:- Bn. H.Q. at L.34.d.3.6. The posts in the front line (extended from M.1.a.3.8 to L.36.a.6.9) being occupied by "B" Coy with their H.Q. at R.5.d.8.8. together with "D" Coy, who remain there in support. "C" Coy are in reserve at L.34.d.3.6. and "A" Coy are in the support trench of the 2/5 S. Staff.	NK

See appendix

Army Form C. 2118

WAR DIARY or INTELLIGENCE SUMMARY

(Erase heading not required.)

2/5 North Stafford Regt.

Volume II. April. 1917.

Place	Date	Hour	Summary of Events and Information	Remarks and references to Appendices
LE VERGUIER	19th	9 p.m.	"A" and "D" Coys relieve "B" Coy occupying front line trenches now that they have been increased. - "D" on the right and "A" on the left. - "B" Coy returning to the support trench recently vacated by "A" Coy. - "A" Coy's new H.Q. being at R.S. F.7.7. CASUALTIES:- NIL.	188
LE VERGUIER	20th	9 p.m.	"A" and "D" Coys carry on wiring and improving their front line of fire trenches. STRENGTH:- 2/Lt E.W.S. THOMAS joined unit. CASUALTIES:- Killed in action:- 2/Lt S. GREVILLE. Sgt Cooper wounded - 1 O.R.	188
-do-	21st	5 p.m.	Bn. H.Q. move to R.H.a.3.3 as their late position is rendered untenable owing to enemy shellfire. "A" and "D" Coys carry on wiring and improving their line of trenches. CASUALTIES:- MISSING:- 1 O.R. (Sergt. Hart)	188
-do-	22nd		Position of the Battalion on morning of 22nd is as follows:- H.Q. at R.H.a.3.3. Front line of trenches being held by "A" and "D" Coys. - "D" Coy holding the right sector with two platoons and H.Q. and 1 platoon in support at R.S.a.88, the left sector being held by 2 platoons of "A" Coy with H.Q. and one Platoon in support at R.S.a.7.7. "C" Coy are in reserve at L.34.d.3.6. and "B" Coy are in support trench of 2/5 South Stafford Regt. at L.34.c.7.7.	188
		10 p.m.	The Bn. is relieved by 2/5 South Stafford Regt. On completion of relief at 1.0 a.m. the following morning "A" and "D" Coys return to billets in JEANCOURT. "B" and "C" Coys remaining	

Army Form C. 2118

WAR DIARY
INTELLIGENCE SUMMARY

(Erase heading not required.)

Volume II April 1917 — 2/5 Bn. North Staffords Regt.

Page 16

Place	Date	Hour	Summary of Events and Information	Remarks and references to Appendices
LE VERGUIER	22nd	10.0 p.m.	Behind to work on erecting and digging trenches on the main line, returning to JEANCOURT before dawn. - Bn. N.Q. being established at L.26.c.7.7. CASUALTIES:- Wounded in action:- 2 O.R.	MS
JEANCOURT	23rd	8.30 p.m.	"A" and "D" Coys leave JEANCOURT to work on the main line returning before dawn the following morning. CASUALTIES:- Wounded in action:- 2 O.R.	MS
—do—	24th	8.30 p.m.	"B" and "C" Coys leave JEANCOURT to work on the main line returning before dawn the following morning. CASUALTIES:- NIL.	MS
—do—	25th	8.30 p.m.	"A" and "D" Coys leave JEANCOURT to work on the main line returning before dawn the following morning. CASUALTIES:- NIL.	MS
—do—	26th	8.30 p.m.	"B" and "C" Coys leave JEANCOURT to work on the main line returning before dawn the following morning. CASUALTIES:- NIL.	MS
—do—	27th	8.30 p.m.	After orders had been received and arrangements made for the Battalion to be relieved by the 2/5 Lincolns Regt. - this order is cancelled and we are ordered to relieve 2/5 South Stafford Regt. holding the front line in the Bde Right Sub-sector. Bn. leaves JEANCOURT to relieve 2/5 South Stafford Regt. "B" and "C" Coys to hold the front line and "A" and "D" Coys in support. Relief was reported complete at 1.5 a.m. the following day. CASUALTIES:- NIL.	MS

Army Form C. 2118

Volume II April 1917
Page 14 — 2/5 Bn North Stafford Regt.

WAR DIARY
INTELLIGENCE SUMMARY
(Erase heading not required.)

Place	Date	Hour	Summary of Events and Information	Remarks and references to Appendices
LE VERGUIER	28th		Dispositions of Bn. on morning of 28th:- Bn HQ. L.33.a.25. The front line trenches 200yds west of wood on G.32. central and trenches previously occupied by this unit from M.1.a.3.8. to L.34.a.6.9 being held by B and C Coys - C on right and B on left - A and D Coys in support, occupying a trench on the Divisional main line of resistance from L.34.c.7.6 to R.5.a.2.8. The 104th Infantry Bde are in touch on our right at M.1.a.7.3 and the 2/6 touch! Staffords 2/5 Lincoln Regt on our left at G.25.c.0.2. In the evening the Bn. was relieved by the 2/5 Lincoln Regt. The relief commencing about 9. p.m and at 1.15 a.m. next day was completed. On relief the Bn. moved to HANCOURT into Divisional Reserve. CASUALTIES:- wounded m{ 1. O.R. action	
HANCOURT	29th		In Divisional Reserve at Hancourt. The Transport and Quartermaster's Stores being at VRAIGNES. CASUALTIES:- NIL.	
HANCOURT	30th		In Divisional Reserve at HANCOURT. CASUALTIES: NIL.	

In the Field
30-4-17

ABonnerman Lieut-Col
Commdg 2/5th North Staff Regt.

Army Form C. 2118.

WAR DIARY
INTELLIGENCE SUMMARY
(Erase heading not required.)

Instructions regarding War Diaries and Intelligence Summaries are contained in F. S. Regs., Part II. and the Staff Manual respectively. Title Pages will be prepared in manuscript.

Vol 4

Confidential

Original

War Diary
of
2/5th North Stafford Regiment

From:- 1st May 1917
To:- 31st May 1917

Place	Date	Hour	Summary of Events and Information	Remarks and references to Appendices

WAR DIARY
or
INTELLIGENCE SUMMARY

(Erase heading not required.)

Army Form C. 2118

Volume II
May 1917.
2/5 Bn. North Stafford Regt.

Place	Date	Hour	Summary of Events and Information	Remarks and references to Appendices
HANCOURT	1st	9.15 am	In Divisional Reserve. Inspection by G.O.C. 176th Infantry Brigade. Training carried out by Battalion.	
-do-	2nd		In Divisional Reserve. Training carried out by Battalion - and Working Parties found.	
-do-	3rd		In Divisional Reserve. Training carried out by Battalion - and Working Parties found.	
-do-	4th		In Divisional Reserve. Training carried out by Battalion - and Working Parties found.	
-do-	5th		In Divisional Reserve. Training carried out by Battalion, and working parties found.	
-do-	6th	7 pm	Battalion leaves HANCOURT on its way to relieve 2/6 Sherwood Foresters in the Brigade right subsector east of HERVILLY. "D" Coy takes over the right sector of the front and "A" Coy the left sector. "B" and "C" Coys being in the outposts on the main line of resistance - C on the right and B on the left. The relief was reported complete at 12.45 am the following day.	

Army Form C. 2118

Volume II - May 1918
Instructions regarding War Diaries and Intelligence
Summaries are contained in F. S. Regs., Part II.
and the Staff Manual respectively. Title Pages
will be prepared in manuscript.

Page ref. _____ 2/5 Br. North Stafford Regt.

WAR DIARY
INTELLIGENCE SUMMARY
(Erase heading not required.)

Place	Date	Hour	Summary of Events and Information	Remarks and references to Appendices
VILLERET.	8		The distribution of the Battalion is as follows:-	
			FRONT LINE - 2 Companies.	
			RIGHT FRONT - "D" Coy. Headquarters:- L.16.A.1.3.	
			Post No 1 - L.18.c.1.2. Post No 2 - L.18.c.3.6. Post No 3 - L.18.a.4.3	
			" 4 - L.18.a.1.7. " B.1. - L.17.A.6.6. B.2. - L.17.A.8.0	
			LEFT FRONT - "A" Coy. Headquarters:- L.10.d.5.4.	
			Post No 5 - L.17.A.5.7. Post No 6 - L.12.c.7.4. Post No 7 - L.11.A.9.5.	
			" 8 - L.11.A.4.1. " 9 - L.11.A.9.5. " 10 - G.7.A.0.5.	
			In touch on right at L.17.d.7.3. and on left at L.11.d.4.1 and	
			Quarry in L.S.d.	
			SUPPORT LINE - 2 Companies.	
			RIGHT SUPPORT - "C" Coy. Headquarters:- L.10.c.8.2.	
			10 posts not yet found up between L.23 a 4.7 and L.10.c.7.2	
			Keeping Whitt 260 yrds of FERVAQUE FARM behind held	
			German wire on the main line of resistance	
			L.G. Post - L.16.c.7.6. Post held at night - L.16.C.5.7.	

WAR DIARY
INTELLIGENCE SUMMARY

Volume II May 1917
2/5 Bn. North Stafford Regt.
Page 20

Army Form C. 2118

Place	Date	Hour	Summary of Events and Information	Remarks and references to Appendices
VILLERET	8		LEFT SUPPORT – "B" Coy – Headquarters – L.10.d.1.6. Old German trench held from L.10.d.1.6. to L.10.a.8.2. with communication trench running into sunken road 200x west. POST: L.10.8.5.2 with communication trench running into sunken road 200x west. BN. H.Q. – L.10.c.6.V. REGT. AID POST – Quarry on L.10.a. central. An ambush was made on the Railway cutting from L.12.a.1 to G.7.6.3.4. by one platoon of "B" Coy. under 2nd Lt. Rosquito. About L.12.a.8.6. no opposition was met until just a small party of Germans were seen to move off at our approach, one of whom was felled by the rifle fire of our men. We received orders for the above operation had been issued, we received orders the platoon he retired to his jumping off place, and at 23 o'clock he re-entered the cutting at the same place. At this time the cutting was found to be occupied and a dug outs were bombed and our men claimed a number of Germans killed. A few Germans	

WAR DIARY
INTELLIGENCE SUMMARY

Volume II May 1917   Army Form C. 2118

2/5th Bn. North Stafford Regt.

Place	Date	Hour	Summary of Events and Information	Remarks and references to Appendices
VILLERET	8		Reached crest of a ridge and had high land in front. The area proved to be untenable owing to enemy fire from G.2.c. central and enemy rifle and M.G. enfilade fire from G.8.a central. The German garrison was estimated to be 30 platoon and had apparently re-occupied the position after our men had occupied the position in the night. Casualties - O.R. 1 killed 5 wounded & missing.	
-do-	9		Arrangements made to repeat the attack on the railway cutting, but owing to the offensive operations which were to have taken place the following day being postponed the attack was cancelled.	
-do-	10		Nil.	
-do-	11		The Battalion was relieved by the 1/5 South Stafford Regt, the relief being complete by 2.10 a.m. the following day. The Batn B.C. & D Coys proceeded into billets in HERVILLY and A Coy into MESNILCOURT in Brigade support.	
HERVILLY	12		Working parties found at night to work on trench line of HERVILLY	
-do-	13		do	do
-do-	14		do	do

Army Form C. 2118

WAR DIARY
or
INTELLIGENCE SUMMARY

(Erase heading not required.)

Volume II May 1917   2/5 Bn. North Stafford Regt.

Place	Date	Hour	Summary of Events and Information	Remarks and references to Appendices
HERNICY	15		The Bn. moves up into the line having HERNICY at 10.0 pm to take over the Brigade right sub-sector from 2/5 South Stafford Regt. As the Battalion to be relieved had to work in the Tunnels until one am. the relief was not complete till 2 am. The following morning (16th).	
VILLERET	16		The distribution of the Battalion was as follows:- BRIGADE SUB-SECTOR RIGHT COY (C) - H.Q. L.16.a.1.3 Posts:- R1.- L.17.d.9.5. R2.- L.18.c.1.6. R3.- L.18.c.1.9. R4.- L.18.a.3.5. Supports:- S.1. L.17.b.9.0. S.2. L.17.9.3. LEFT COY (B) H.Q.- L.10.d.8.4. Posts- R5.- L.18.a.5.8. R6.L.12.c.7.1. R7.L.12.c.7.3. R8. L.12.c.6.7 - This post has yet to be dug. R9. L.11.d.9.7. S.3. L.17.4.8.9. Supports - in VILLERET. New Coy HQ to be made at:- RIGHT FRONT COY - L.17.b.9.3 } to be completed. LEFT - L.11.d.7.6. }	

Volume II - May 1917

Instructions regarding War Diaries and Intelligence Summaries are contained in F.S. Regs, Part II and the Staff Manual respectively. Title Pages will be prepared in manuscript.

Army Form C. 2118

2/5 Bn. North Staffs Regt

WAR DIARY
INTELLIGENCE SUMMARY
(Erase heading not required.)

Place	Date	Hour	Summary of Events and Information	Remarks and references to Appendices
VILLERET	16		Right Support Coy (D) H.Q. - L.10.c.6.6. Left Support Coy (B) H.Q. L.10.c.8.2. Right Support Coy (A) H.Q. L.10.d.1.6. Battalion H.Q. - L.10.c.6.6. Regt Aid Post - Quarry L.10.a.4.6. Dumps: Bn. S.A.A. Grenade & R.E. dump - L.17.a.6.5. Right Coy R.E. dumps - L.17.b.9.5. L.17.b.9.9. Left " " " L.15.d.8.8. Field Kitchens and water carts are brought up during the night and taken back to Quarry in L.13.d.9. on before dawn. Kitchens are brought to: L.17.b.9.0. for the Right front Coy. L.17.b.9.8. " " Left " " L.15.d.8.8. " " { Right Support Coy { Regt. Water carts are brought to: L.17.b.9.0. for the 2 front Coys L.15.d.6.8. " " 2 support " In touch on the flanks at: Right flank - L.24.a.9.3. Left " - L.11.d.5.5.	

Army Form C. 2118

WAR DIARY
or
INTELLIGENCE SUMMARY

Volume II - May 1917

2/5 Bn Royal Stafford Regt

(Erase heading not required.)

Instructions regarding War Diaries and Intelligence Summaries are contained in F.S. Regs., Part II. and the Staff Manual respectively. Title Pages will be prepared in manuscript.

Place	Date	Hour	Summary of Events and Information	Remarks and references to Appendices
VILLERET	17		In Brigade Right subsector - front line.	Casualties:- 1 O.R. killed.
do	18		— do —	Casualties:- 1 O.R. wounded
do	19		— do —	
do	20		The Battalion was relieved by the 2/5 South Stafford Regt but as work had to be carried out at the defences until 1 am the following morning the relief was not reported complete till 4.5 am. On completion of relief the Battalion returned to billets - A. B. & C. in HERVILLY and D Coy in HESBECOURT	
HERVILLY	21		In Bde support.	
do	22		The Bn. found working parties to work on main line of Resistance.	
do	23		The Bn. moved to the Quarries N.E of TEMPLEUX in F.27.c. after being relieved by 2nd Bengal Lancers. The Bn. S. arrived about 3.30 pm and we came correspondents the orders of the 2nd Cavalry Division.	

Army Form C. 2118

Volume II — May 1917

Page 28

Instructions regarding War Diaries and Intelligence Summaries are contained in F. S. Regs., Part II. and the Staff Manual respectively. Title Pages will be prepared in manuscript.

WAR DIARY
INTELLIGENCE SUMMARY

2/5 North Stafford Regt

(Erase heading not required.)

Place	Date	Hour	Summary of Events and Information	Remarks and references to Appendices
TEMPLEUX	24		Bn. Transferred to 2nd Cavalry Division, and working at wiring intermediate line during the night	
do	25		do	
do	26		do	
do	27		do	
do	28		do	
do	29		do Casualties 1 O.R. wounded	
do	30		Bn. moves to HAMELET and joins 176th Brigade agreeing in HAMELET 1.30 p.m. Casualties 1 O.R. accidentally wounded.	
HAMELET	31		Bn. move to EQUANCOURT to join the remainder of the Brigade and rejoin the 59th Division in XV Corps area — marching via HEZECOURT - LECHELLE & NURLU; distance 8½ miles arrival 9.40 p.m. Transport and Q.M. Stores move from ROISEL and arrives at EQUANCOURT	

Harry Johnson
Lt. Col.
2/5 N Staff Regt

Army Form C. 2118.

WAR DIARY
or
INTELLIGENCE SUMMARY

(Erase heading not required.)

Vol 5

Confidential

2/5th N.S.

War Diary
of
2/5th North Stafford Regiment

From 1st June 1917
To 30th June 1917

Original

Volume I June 1917

Page 26   2/5 Bn North Stafford Regt

Army Form C. 2118.

WAR DIARY
INTELLIGENCE SUMMARY

(Erase heading not required.)

Hour, Date, Place	Summary of Events and Information	Remarks and references to Appendices
EQUANCOURT 1st	In Divisional Reserve. — Strength 41 Officers 723 O.R. Kitchen fatigues carried out and working parties found for Brigade Buildings	
2nd	In Divisional Reserve. — Working parties carried out	
3rd	— do —	
4th	— do —	
5th	— do —	
6th	— do —	
7th	— do — Inspection of Company by G.O.C. Lucknow Inf. Bde.	
8th	Party at work on road between EQUANCOURT and ETRICOURT	
9th	In Divisional Reserve. Working Party found	
10th	— do —	

Army Form C. 2118.

Volume II June 1917
Page 24

Instructions regarding War Diaries and Intelligence Summaries are contained in F.S. Regs., Part II and the Staff Manual respectively. Title pages will be prepared in manuscript.

WAR DIARY
or
INTELLIGENCE SUMMARY.
(Erase heading not required.)

— 2/5 Bn North Stafford Regt

Place	Hour, Date	Summary of Events and Information	Remarks and references to Appendices
EQUANCOURT	11th	Battalion leaves EQUANCOURT at 9.35 p.m. in order to relieve 2/5 Notts & Derby Regt holding the right sub-sector, Left Bde. 59th Divisional front. Battalion marched via FINS and METZ carrying the advance line at 9.45 p.m. Relief reported complete at 1.15 a.m. O.M. Stores and Transport move to YPRES. Army encampment at VAULSBERT WOOD Q.27.L.23	[illegible]
BEAUCAMP	12th	Disposition of the Battalion is as follows. A and D Companies in the front line - A on the left and D on the right. (About 150 yards in front of the old line there is an advanced line in charge of 5 posts) B Coy are in reserve and C Coy in support in the intermediate line. Position of H.H. Q.27.f.26. 3rd Aid Post in Quarry at R.16.c.21. Work carried out during the night forming up the advanced posts to make them into a continuous line.	[illegible]

Volume I - June 1917

Army Form C. 2118.

Page 28

2/5- Bn North Stafford

WAR DIARY
or
INTELLIGENCE SUMMARY.
(Erase heading not required.)

Hour, Date, Place		Summary of Events and Information	Remarks and references to Appendices
BEAUCAMP	13	Work continued during the night on advanced posts. No horse belonging to Field Kitchen was killed by rifle fire.	
	14	Our patrol, consisting of 1 N.C.O. and 5 men was attacked and beaten off by a strong German patrol which was lying in ambush just outside our wire. Casualties - 1 killed (1 man) and 3 wounded. Work continued during the night on the advanced posts.	
	15	Work continued during the night on advanced posts - Casualties - 1 O.R. died of wounds.	
	16	do. do.	do.
	17	do. do.	Casualties: 3 O.R. wounded & 1 accidentally wounded
	18	do. do.	do.
	19	do. do.	do.
	20	Joining up of advanced posts completed.	do.
	21	Improving and wiring new front line & Trench commenced between new front line and forward support line.	do.

Army Form C. 2118.

WAR DIARY
or
INTELLIGENCE SUMMARY.

(Erase heading not required.)

Volume I June 1917
Page 29

2/5 Bn North Stafford Regt

Hour, Date, Place	Summary of Events and Information	Remarks and references to Appendices
BEAUCAMP 22.	Battalion relieved by 2/5 South Stafford Regt – less "B" Coy which remains in reserve under the orders of 2/5 South Stafford Regt.	
23.	On completion of relief Battalion moves to METZ. The men occupying the second line trench.	
	In Bde support at METZ. Working Parties found at night to work on C.T. to front line.	
24	-do-	
25	-do-	
26	Transport moves back. MT stores to R & a bn alter.	
27	-do- Working Party -do- C.T.	
	employed on C.T.	
METZ 28	In Brigade support at METZ. "B" Coy in the line relieved by a Company of 2/5 South Stafford Regt and returned to occupy trenches in METZ.	

Volume II - June 1917

Army Form C. 2118.

WAR DIARY

INTELLIGENCE SUMMARY

2/5 North Stafford Regt

(Erase heading not required.)

*Instructions regarding War Diaries and Intelligence Summaries are contained in F. S. Regs., Part II. and the Staff Manual respectively. Title pages will be prepared in manuscript.

Hour, Date, Place	Summary of Events and Information	Remarks and references to Appendices
METZ. 29	In Bde Support at METZ. Working parties found for work on C.T. Casualties :- 1 o.r. wounded.	NSS
30	do	NSS

F.C. Mecenery
Major
Comdg 2/5-North Stafford Regt

Army Form C. 2118.

WAR DIARY
or
INTELLIGENCE SUMMARY

(Erase heading not required.)

17/39

Job 6

Confidential

War Diary
of
25th No. North Stafford Regiment

From:- July 1st 1917
To July 31st 1917

Original

Volume II – July 1917

Army Form C. 2118.

WAR DIARY
or
INTELLIGENCE SUMMARY.
(Erase heading not required.)

Page 3/ will be prepared in manuscript. — 2/5 North Stafford Regt —

Hour, Date, Place		Summary of Events and Information	Remarks and references to Appendices
METZ.	1st	Battalion moves to EQUANCOURT on relief by 2/5 Leicesters in Divisional Reserve.	(A/1)
EQUANCOURT	2nd	In Divisional Reserve. Bath parties arrived at —	(A/1) (B/1)
	3rd	— do — — do —	(A/1) (B/1)
	4th	— do — — do —	(A/1) (B/1)
	5th	— do — — do —	(A/1)
	6th	— do — — do —	(A/1)
	7th	Battalion moves to BARASTRE to occupy camp at O.10.c.27. on relief by 58th Division. Route of march via LECHELLE and RMS. Time of arrival 8.30 a.m.	(A/1)
BARASTRE.	8th	In Army Reserve. Bn. training carried out	(A/1)
	9th	— do — — do —	(A/1)

Army Form C. 2118.

WAR DIARY
or
INTELLIGENCE SUMMARY.
2/5 North Stafford Regt
(Erase heading not required.)

Volume II. July 1917

Instructions regarding War Diaries and Intelligence Summaries are contained in F.S. Regs., Part II. and the Staff Manual respectively. Title pages will be prepared in manuscript.

Place	Date	Hour	Summary of Events and Information	Remarks and references to Appendices
BARASTRE	10		Bn. in Army Reserve. Training Carried out.	
	11		- do - - do -	
	12		- do - - do -	
	13		- do - - do -	
	14		- do - Battalion Sports.	
	15		- do - Training carried out.	
	16		- do - - do -	
	17		- do - Brigade training carried out.	
	18		- do - - do -	
	19		- do - Battalion training carried out.	
	20		- do - - do -	

Volume II July 1917
Page 133

WAR DIARY
or
INTELLIGENCE SUMMARY. 2/5 Bn. North Stafford Regt.

Army Form C. 2118.

Hour, Date, Place	Summary of Events and Information	Remarks and references to Appendices
BARASTRE.		
21st	In Army Reserve. Having what 11 aims took place during remainder of day.	
22nd	In Army Reserve. Battalion training.	
23rd	-do-	
24th	-do-	
25th	-do-	
26th	-do-	
27th	-do-	
28th	-do- Brigade Field Day — training.	
29th	-do- Battalion training.	
30th	-do-	
31st	-do- Brigade training.	

Hay Gulliver Lt-Col.
C.md. 2/5 North Stafford Regt.

Army Form C. 2118.

WAR DIARY
or
INTELLIGENCE SUMMARY
(Erase heading not required.)

Confidential

Places	Date	Hour	Summary of Events and Information	Remarks and references to Appendices
Original			War Diary of 2/5th Bn North Staffordshire Regiment From 1st August 1917 To 31st August 1917	

Volume 2. August 1917

Page 34

Army Form C. 2118.

WAR DIARY
or
INTELLIGENCE SUMMARY.
(Erase heading not required.)

Hour, Date, Place		Summary of Events and Information	Remarks and references to Appendices
BARASTRE:	1st	In Army Reserve - Battalion training. Col. Sir A.B. announces strength.	WSR
	2nd	Do	Battalion training	WSR
	3rd	Do	Battalion training	WSR
	4th	Do	Divisional Tactical Exercise near SAILLY-SAILLISEL. Lieut. Grinnell was sent unless struck off strength. Capt. Isadore Ramsay attached to unit vice Capt. M. (small res.) Drafts of 1 N.C.O. and 19 O.R. arrived from 12 & 9 D. CALAIS	WSR
	5th	Do	Attestation following 476th Brigade A.D.V.S. - IV Corps inspected 476th Brigade Transport on 30/7/17 - he reports "Inspected this morning the horses of the 176th Brigade. Their excellent condition reflects great credit on the work of Transport Officers"	WSR

Volume 2 August 1917
Page 35.

WAR DIARY
or
INTELLIGENCE SUMMARY.
(Erase heading not required.)

Army Form C. 2118.

Hour, Date, Place		Summary of Events and Information	Remarks and references to Appendices
BARASTRE	5th In Army Reserve.	All those concerned. I also noticed in these Units great progress in the erection of horse standings. (Sd) C.D.M. HARRIS Lt Col A.D.V.S. IV CORPS The Corps Commander records with satisfaction the contents of the above Report and wishes that all concerned should be so informed	WSA
	6th Do	Battalion Training	WSA
	7th Do	Battalion Training	WSA
	8th Do	Battalion Training - G.O.C. Brigade inspected Camp.	WSA
	9th Do	Battalion Training - "A" and "D" Companies field firing	WSA
	10th Do	Battalion Sports - Draft 9 2 N.COs + 7 ORs from CALAIS	WSA
	11th Do	Battalion Training	WSA
	12th Do	Draft 9 29 ORs from ETAPLES	WSA

Volume 2 - August 1917
Page 36

Army Form C. 2118.

WAR DIARY
or
INTELLIGENCE SUMMARY.
(Erase heading not required.)

Place	Hour, Date	Summary of Events and Information	Remarks and references to Appendices
BARASTRE	13th	In Army Reserve - Brigade Sports -	WSR
	14th	Do Battalion training	WSR
	15th	Do Do	WSR
	16th	Do 4 Cadets from CALAIS. Battalion training - Brigadier General T.G. Cope D.S.O. assumes command of the Brigade vice Brigadier General R.a. Anne D.S.O.	WSR
	17th	Do Battalion training CALAIS	WSR
	18th	Do 4 Cadets from CALAIS Battalion training	WSR
	19th	Do Battalion Church Parade.	WSR
	20th	Do Battalion training Calais - Major 14 ORs from Calais - 2Lieut WSa Pullen struck off strength	WSR
	21st	Do Battalion training - Major 9, 1 NCO & 59 ORs from ETAPLES	WSR

Volume 2. August 1917
Page 37

WAR DIARY
or
INTELLIGENCE SUMMARY.
(Erase heading not required.)

Army Form C. 2118.

Hour, Date, Place			Summary of Events and Information	Remarks and references to Appendices
BARASTRE	22nd	In Army Reserve.	Battalion training. Draft of N.C.Os & O.Rs from CALAIS	WM
	23rd	do	The 59th Division moved to the district from BOUZINCOURT to ACHEUX, this Battalion being "eye-witnessed" billets at FORCEVILLE. The Battalion marched	WM
BARASTRE AND FORCÉVILLE			to a point about one mile south-east of LE SARS, on the BAPAUME-ALBERT Road. At this point the Battalion entrained, and the remainder of the journey was done by bus.	
FORCÉVILLE	24th	do	Battalion Route March -	WM
	25th	do	Battalion Route March	WM
	26th	do	Voluntary Church Parades.	WM
	27th	do	Battalion Route March: Draft of 32 O.R. ex CALAIS	WM

Volume 2. August 1917

Page 38

Instructions regarding War Diaries and Intelligence Summaries are contained in F.S. Regs., Part II. and the Staff Manual respectively. Title pages will be prepared in manuscript.

Army Form C. 2118.

WAR DIARY
or
INTELLIGENCE SUMMARY.
(Erase heading not required.)

Hour, Date, Place		Summary of Events and Information	Remarks and references to Appendices
FORCEVILLE	28th	In Army Reserve. Battalion Training - 2/Lt Peach was accidentally wounded by rifle Hand Grenade. Advance party 1 Officer + ORs left for Warloy area.	WDR
	29th		Battalion Route March.	WDR
	30th		Ordered to move to new area. Was subsequently postponed for 24 hours. Battalion Route March.	WDR
	31st		Three Companies (B, C, + D) and Transport entrained at AVELUY for new area, departing at 2.11pm. "A" Company + Field Kitchens detailed to leave for new area 12 hours later.	WDR

Harry Gilman
Lieut - Col
Commanding 2/5 North Staff: Regt.

Army Form C. 2118.

WAR DIARY
or
INTELLIGENCE SUMMARY.
(Erase heading not required.)

17/59

Vol 8

Original   Confidential

War Diary

of

2/5th Bn North Stafford Regiment

From: Sept 1st 1917.
To: Sept 30th 1917.

Volume 2
September
~~August~~ 1917
Page 39

Instructions regarding War Diaries and Intelligence
Summaries are contained in F.S. Regs., Part II.
and the Staff Manual respectively. Title pages
will be prepared in manuscript.

WAR DIARY
or
~~INTELLIGENCE SUMMARY.~~
(Erase heading not required.)

2/5 N. Staff Regt.

Army Form C. 2118.

Hour, Date, Place	Summary of Events and Information	Remarks and references to Appendices
WINNIZEELE 1st	In Army Reserve. Arrived at HOPOUTRE at 2 a.m. Marched 11 miles to new area arriving at 7 a.m. "A" Company detrained at HOPOUTRE at 7 p.m. and proceeded to new area	WR
2nd	Do. "A" Company arrived at new area at 2 a.m.	WR
3rd	Do. Battalion training	WR
4th	Do. [illegible] Company training	WR
5th	Do. Battalion training afternoon	
6th	Do. Company training. Battalion training	
7th	Do. Company & Platoon training. Rifle shoots in the afternoon	
8th	Do. Battalion training	
9th	Do. Church Parades	

Volume Re.2 September 1917.   2/5th N. Staff Regt.   Army Form C. 2118.

WAR DIARY
or
INTELLIGENCE SUMMARY
(Erase heading not required.)

Hour, Date, Place	Summary of Events and Information	Remarks and references to Appendices
WINNIZEELE 10th	In Army Reserve. Brigade Route March about 10 mile.	AA
11th	Ditto. Battalion Training (Light work)	AA
12th	Ditto. Company Training	AA
13th	Ditto. Battalion Training	AA
14th	Ditto. Individual & Platoon Training.	AA
15th	Ditto. Brigade Welfare	AA
16th	Ditto. Church Parades	AA
17th	Ditto. Brigade Operations.	AA
18th	Ditto. Company Training.	AA
19th	The 176th Inf. Bde. moved to BRANDHOEK by Motor Lorries, the entraining taking place on the road to STEENVOORDE about 2 miles S.E. of WINNIZEELE and debussing near POPPERINGHE from where the Battalion had to march to DERBY CAMP, BRANDHOEK. The transport moved by road via POPPERINGHE arriving at DERBY CAMP at noon. The battalion left WINNIZEELE at 10·40 PM and arrived at BRANDHOEK at BRANDHOEK about 5·0 PM under canvas.	AA

"Volume 2" September 1917.   2/5th N. Stafford Regt.

WAR DIARY
INTELLIGENCE SUMMARY
(Erase heading not required.)

Army Form C. 2118.

Instructions regarding War Diaries and Intelligence Summaries are contained in F.S. Regs., Part II and the Staff Manual respectively. Title pages will be prepared in manuscript.

Page 41.

Hour, Date, Place	Summary of Events and Information	Remarks and references to Appendices
BRANDHOEK. September 20th	Interior & Platoon Training. The Commanding Officer & the four Company Commanders proceeded up the line in the afternoon to reconnoitre the ground East of WIELTZE then being held by the 55th Div.	188.
" YPRES NORTH. 21st	In Reserve to the 55th Division & under orders to move forward at a moment's notice. Copy of G.O.O. 2042 on the events of a move are attached. During the afternoon orders are received to move forward to YPRES NORTH Camp. Hd A.932 and that Lt. Col. H. Johnson would assume command of the Battalion and not Major O.C. Boden as stated in orders. The Battalion and transport and baggage detailed to be left behind as detailed in S.S. 135 "Instructions for the Training of Divisions for Offensive Actions" Chap'r XXI & armaments arrived at YPRES NORTH at 6.0pm, all transport & above mentioned personnel remained behind in DERBY CAMP.	188. Map Reference Sheet 29 NW. Edit 5A. 1/20000 attached - B.O.O. 42. Appendix 1. " " 43. " " 2.
YPRES NORTH. 22nd	In Reserve to the 55th Division. 1 officer and 2 runners per company go forward to reconnoitre the ground	188.
" 23rd	In Reserve to the 55th Division. During the afternoon orders are received that 176th Inf Bde would relieve the 164th & 165th Inf Bde. 55th Div. during the night of 23/24th. The 2/5th N. Staff. Regt. relieving the 2 Battalions of the 164th Inf Bde in support on the right. B.O.O. attached of the relief together with armaments. Completion of relief was reported at 1.0 AM next morning. Transport & baggage left behind in DERBY CAMP move to a Bde Camp for details at H8A 4.3.	188. attached - B.O.O. 44. Appendix 3. Armaments " " 4.

(73989) W4141—463. 400,000. 9/14. H.&J.Ltd. Forms/C. 2118/10.

WAR DIARY or INTELLIGENCE SUMMARY

Army Form C. 2118.

Volume 2. September 1917.   2/5th N. Staff Regt.

Page 42

Hour, Date, Place	Summary of Events and Information	Remarks and references to Appendices
SEPTEMBER		
East of WIELTJE — 24th	Dispositions of the Battn. on the morning of the 24th were:— Battn. Hdqtrs at CAPRICORN KEEP, C.18.D.57; two companies "B" + "C" being in support at C.18.B.4.2 and DONT TRENCH, D.13.C.14 respectively and two in reserve "A" Coy at C.23.C.77 in CALL RESERVE and CALL SUPPORT Trenches and "D" Coy at C.23.C.83 in CAMBRAI RESERVE Trench. In the afternoon orders were received that the 176th Inf. Bde. would be relieved at night the 24/25th by the 177th and 178th Inf. Bdes, the 175th Inf. Bde. being in Bde and the 2/5th N. Staff being relieved by the 7/8 and the 25th Sherwoods, completion of relief being reported at 12.15 AM the 25th. On completion of relief the Battalion marched to YPRES & St Jean to being billeted in cellars. Battalion Hdqts being established at I.7.C.97. Casualties 2 O.R.S Killed and 2 wounded.	Reference maps. Sheet 28 N.W.2 -- 1/10000 28 N.E.1 -- 1/10000 Reference map Sheet 28 N.W. -- 1/20000
YPRES — 25th	Orders having been received that the 2/5th N. Staff Regt would be attached as battalion in Reserve to the 178th Inf. Bde. for the attack on the 26th September, 4 scout assembled in CAPRICORN TRENCHES C+C the Battalion moves off from YPRES at midnight 25/26th to CAPRICORN TRENCHES where it assembles ready for the attack at dawn on the 26th.	Reference map Sheet 28 N.W.2 -- 1/10000
East of WIELTJE — 26th	Dispositions of the Battn. when the Bombardment previous to the attack commenced at 3.50 A.M on the 26th were:— Battn Headquarters at C.18.D.31 behind La German Pill Box, "A" + "Q" Coys being on the first line and "B" + "C" in support, "A" + "B" on the left + "C" + "D" on the right of the WIELTJE — GRAVENSTAFEL Road, H.M.P. at Battn Hdqts, B.O.0.13 at. 47 attached.	Ditto. Attached S.O. 47 Appendix 5.

Volume 2 September 1917

Army Form C. 2118.

WAR DIARY
or
INTELLIGENCE SUMMARY. 1/5th N. Stafford Regt.

(Erase heading not required.)

Page 43

Hour, Date, Place	Summary of Events and Information	Remarks and references to Appendices
SEPTEMBER		
East of WIELTJE 26th (cont'd)	Zero hour was at 5-50 AM and until 11-30 AM the Battalion remained in its forming up place CAPRICORN TRENCHES, at about 11-30 AM Companies commenced to move forward and take up new position about KEIR FARM in D.13.D, at 2-35 PM. Battn. Headquarters were moved forward and established behind POND FARM, C.18.B.70.02, the A.P. moving to this new position. Disposition of the Battalion on the morning of the 26th were as under:— Battn Hdqrs + RAP — POND FARM, C.18.B.70.02. 'B' Coy holding a line north & north of D.13.A.9.2, 'C', 'D' & 'A' Coy holding a line GALLIPOLI, D.13.D.4.1. to D.13.D.5.9. During the day and about 5-0 PM previous to a counter attack the enemy put down very heavy artillery barrages causing a good many casualties. Rations water & totten was fetched and distributed with shar made about 6 were brought up as far as SPREE FARM at 6-0 PM on pack horses, from where they were fetched by carrying parties. Disposition of the Battalion at noon on the 27th were:— Battn Hdqrs + RAP — POND FARM. 'A' Coy — KANSAS CROSS, D14.7.1.3, 'B' Coy — D.13.A.5.2, 'C' 'D' Coys — KEIR FARM D.13.D.8.4."	Reference Maps Sheet 28.N.E.1 — 1/10000
" — " 27th	During the afternoon orders were received that the Battalion would assemble in the vicinity of SPREE FARM as soon as dark for the purpose of finding carrying parties & completion of carrying & would return to the O.O. GERMAN FRONT LINE Trench at C.28.C.96.24 from Zero Hr 176th D.B.I. H.Q.	Reference Maps Sheet 28.N.W.2 — 1/10000

WAR DIARY or INTELLIGENCE SUMMARY

Army Form C. 2118.

Volume I. September 1917
Page 414

2nd N. Staff Bn.

Hour, Date, Place	Summary of Events and Information	Remarks and references to Appendices
SEPTEMBER		
East of WIELTJE -- 27th (cont)	Owing to an enemy counter-attack taking place at dusk this move was postponed and at 7.54 PM one company "B" was ordered to move forward and clear up the situation. a counter-attack of our line had been limited but finally they were not required. They remained at KANSAS CROSS, D.14.A.11. At 10.0 PM, "A", "C" & "D" Coys were ordered to assemble at CAPRICORN TRENCHES and commence to carry up S.A.A. rations and water to the 4 Battalion of the 173rd Inf. Bde. and at the same time orders were received from the 118th Inf. Bde. for "B" Coy then at KANSAS CROSS to move to MARTHA HOUSE D.14.c.96 in support to the Right Battalion of the Brigade but the guide sent two small to find this way to the Company remained at KANSAS CROSS until they received orders direct from the 178th Inf. Bde. to return to CAPRICORN TRENCHES and given the Battalion Dump and the R.A.P. moved back to SPREE FARM C.18.D.31. at 11.20 PM & orders were then received to remain there till dawn on the 28th in case of any enemy counter-attack but at 3.0 AM on the 28th orders were received to move back to CALL RESERVE TRENCHES & again the 176th Inf. Bd., "B" Coy arriving at SPREE FARM just as the Battalion moved off.	Reference map. Sheet 28 N.E.1 ... 1/10000.
" 28th	At 6.15 AM on the 28th Battalion Headquarters had moved & were established at CALL FARM, C.23.C.17. The four Companies being in CALL RESERVE and CALL SUPPORT Trenches. About noon orders were received that the Battalion would move after dusk to VLAMERTINGHE and at 9.30 PM the 2nd OTAGO Battalion, 2nd NEW ZEALAND Bde. arrived to relieve the Battalion	Reference map. Sheet 28 N.W.2 ... 1/10000.

Army Form C. 2118.

WAR DIARY
or
INTELLIGENCE SUMMARY

2/7 R. Highland Regt.

Volume 2. September 1917
Page 45

(Erase heading not required.)

Instructions regarding War Diaries and Intelligence Summaries are contained in F.S. Regs., Part II and the Staff Manual respectively. Title Pages will be prepared in manuscript.

Place	Date Sept	Hour	Summary of Events and Information	Remarks and references to Appendices
East of WIELTJE	28"	(cont'd)	But as "A" & "D" Coys had to act as carrying parties to the 2/5 & 2/6 SHERWOODS to carry up S.A.A., rations & water to the front line relief was not reported complete until 11.15 p.m. On completion of relief companies were ordered to march, a 100 yds interval being maintained between platoons. Wieltje to YPRES Station, H12 D95 tram the main YPRES Rd with. Tea orders to entrain there for VLAMERTINGHE at 3.0 AM but after waiting two or three hours till 3-30 AM and no train arrived they were ordered to march to VLAMERTINGHE where they were billeted on huts at H9 C47 arriving there about 5.0 AM on the 29"	Reference Map Sheet 28 NW 1/20000
VLAMERTINCHE	29"		Two battalions of the 176th Inf Bde move to the WATOU AREA. The 2/5" N. Staff Regt moving off in motor lorries from VLAMERTINGHE at 4-30 PM. The transport moving by road at 1-0 PM. These Coys are encamped at HOWE CAMP, K11 C9.3 and one coy in a farm near to. The battalion arriving at 6.0 PM.	Reference Map Sheet 27 4/100,000
WATOU	30"		Saturday. Church parades, during the evening orders are received that the 39th Division would be moving to the STEENBECQUE Area on the 1st October. The 2/5" R. Staff Regt moving by motor bus.	

CASUALTIES for 26", 27", 28":

Officers

Killed: 2nd Lt T.F. Rathbone 26-9-17

Other Ranks

Killed — 18.

Wounded — 119.

Missing — 3.

Wounded Capt J. Hodgkinson 26-9-17
" 2nd Lt H.E. Sass "
" J.H. Worrall "
" E.M. Cohen "
" F.W. Lovehope 25-9-17
Wounded remaining at duty
(gas)

Wounded remaining at duty
2nd Lt E. Carhart 26-9-17
" E.W. Thomas 24-9-17

Harry Dillman Lieut Col
Comdg 2/7 R.H. Highland Regt

In the Field
3-10-17

APPENDIX 1

SECRET.   BATTALION OPERATION ORDERS No. 42,   (Copy for War
                       - by -   Diary).
              LIEUT-COL. H. JOHNSON,
                   Commanding   In the Field,
           2/5th Bn. NORTH STAFFORD REGIMENT.   21st Sept, 1917.

Map ref. 28 N.W. 1/10000 and 1/20000.
----

1. The Battalion will prepare to move to YPRES NORTH Area, H.11.b.1.3.

2. Transport and Q.M. Stores will remain in the present Camp, together with the list of other ranks forwarded to Companies on Septr. 12th under this Office letter B.12, also the following Officers:-

      Lieut-Col. H. Johnson.
      Capt. W. N. Bladen.
      2/Lt. R. M. Trimble.

Names of other ranks left behind will be forwarded to Bn. Orderly Room by 9 a.m.

3. Major O. C. Bladen will command the 2/5th North Staffs Regt.

4. Dress and equipment will be as in Chapter XXI, S.S.135, subject to the following amendments:-

1. Officers' Dress will be exactly the same as their men.
2. The pack will be carried, and not the haversack.
   All surplus kit of men will be packed in sandbags, labelled with Regtl. No., Rank, Name, Platoon and Regt, and left at Quartermaster's Stores.
3. The following articles will be carried in the pack:-
   1 Iron Ration.
   Unexpended portion of day's rations.
   1 Bandolier S.A.A.
   Waterproof sheet.
   1 Pair Socks.
   Mess Tin.
   Spare Oil Tin.
   Knife, fork and spoon.
4. Ammunition, 170 rounds, including 50 rounds in pack, except in the case of Rifle Grenadiers, Signallers, Scouts, Runners, Lewis Gunners, and Carrying Parties, who will only carry 50 rounds.
5. Rifle Grenadiers will carry 10 rifle grenades in 2 S.A.A. bandoliers.
6. Bombing and Rifle Sections will carry 2 hand or "P" grenades per man, one in each pocket. 4 "P" Grenades will be carried per section.
7. All men except Nos. 1 and 2 of Lewis Guns, and Runners, will carry a pick or shovel, in the proportion of 1 pick to 4 shovels. Men carrying pick or shovel will pack their entrenching tool with their spare kit.
8. Each man will carry 2 RED Aeroplane flares, also 2 sandbags.
9. "B" and "C" Coys will carry 16 S.O.S. signals, and "A" and "D" Coys will carry 8.
10. Men equipped with the 1" Very pistols will carry 6 cartridges. 2 Very Pistols will be carried per Company.
11. 2 Watsons Fans, if available, will be carried per Platoon, for communicating with Aeroplanes.
12. Platoon Identity Discs will be carried by Platoons.
13. Water bottles will be filled.
14. Mopping up bands will be carried by "D" Coy in the pockets, and Carrying Bands by "A" Coy in the pockets.
15. 16 Wirecutters will be carried by "B" and "C" Coys and 8 each by "A" and "D" Coys. The wirecutters will be attached to the mens shoulder strap by a string and the cutters tucked into the waistbelt.
    Men equipped with wirecutters or wire breakers will wear a piece of whitetape tied to the shoulder straps.

(Contd).

5. **Supplies.** In the event of Units moving, supplies will be delivered to Quartermaster's Stores direct by Divisional Train.

6. Surplus 1" and 1½" Very Pistols will be returned to Q.M. Stores.

7. **Maps, etc.** Attention is drawn to S.S.135, Chapter 33.
Map and Message form may be obtained from Bn. Orderly Room.

8. **Transport.** Water carts, Lewis Gun Limbers, and Field Kitchens, will proceed with the Battalion. Water Carts can be filled at VLAMERTINGHE. The remainder of the Transport will draw S.A.A., "P" Bombs, Grenades Hand and Rifle, Aeroplane flares, S.O.S. Signals, Very Light cartridges 1" from 55th Divisional Main Grenade Dump, H.8.a.4.0., and Sandbags, shovels and picks, from R.E. Dump at H.8.a.5.0., and will proceed to H.11.b.1.3. and report to Bn. H.Q.
Petrol tins will be filled.
On unloading Transport will return to present Camp.

9. **Dumps.** The following Table shews Dumps in 55th Divisional Area:-

Divisional Main Grenade Dump - H.8.a.4.0. (500 yds West of VLAMERTINGHE)

Divisional Emergency Grenade Dump. ST. JEAN.

Divisional R.E. Main Dump. H.8.a.5.0.

Divisional R.E. Emergency Dump. ST JEAN - WIELTJE Rd (600 yds West of WIELTJE).

Right Brigade.

Brigade Dump - C.20.a.8.0. (On North side of No. 5 Track).

Advanced Dumps - BANK FARM, C.24.b.3.6.
POMMERN CASTLE, D.19.a.4.3.

Left Brigade.

Brigade Dump - C.23.c.3.1. (Junction of old German Front Line and WIELTJE - GRAVENSTAFEL Road).
Advanced Dumps - WINE HOUSE.   C.18.c.6.0.
POND FARM.   C.18.d.8.0.
SPREE FARM.   c C.18.d.5.3.
Dug-outs at   C.18.d.7.5.
SOMME.   C.13.c.5.4.

10. Acknowledge.

(Sd) V. B. SHELLEY, Capt.
Adjt. 2/5th North Staffs Regt.

Issued at 12.45 a.m.

Distribution - NORMAL.

AMENDMENTS TO BN. OPERATION ORDERS No. 42.

The following alterations in the Grenades carried by Bombers and Rifle Grenadiers will take place to-morrow morning; all surplus grenades to be returned to the R.S.M. who will arrange to return them to the Dump.
(1) Rifle and Bombing Sections will only carry 1 hand grenade per man.
(2) Rifle Grenadiers will only carry 5 Rifle Grenades.

22/9/17.

(Sd) V. B. SHELLEY, Capt.
Adjt. 2/5th North Staffs Regt.

APPENDIX 2

BATTALION OPERATION ORDERS No. 43,   (Copy for War Diary).
- by -
LIEUT-COL. H. JOHNSON,
Commanding   In the Field,
2/5th Bn. NORTH STAFFORD REGIMENT.   21st Sept, 1917.

1. The remainder of the 176th Inf. Bde. will remove to YPRES NORTH Area this afternoon.

2. The Battalion (less Transport and personnel already detailed to remain behind) will parade ready to move off in the order A, B, C, D. The head of the column will be opposite Bn. Orderly Room at 3.45 p.m.
    Intervals of 100 yards will be maintained between Platoons.
    Headquarters Coy will parade at the head of the Battalion and will move forward at the head of "A" Coy's No. 1 Platoon.

3. The under-mentioned Transport will be ready to move off at 3.45 p.m.
    4 Lewis Gun Limbers.
    4 Field Kitchens.
    Officers' Chargers.
    Os.C. Companies will see that their Yukon Packs are carried on their Lewis Gun Limbers.
    Transport will return to the present Camp on completion of move.

4. Companies will send their C.Q.M.Sgts. to report to 2/Lt. T. Bassett at once to proceed on in advance to arrange accommodation.

                              (Sd) V. B. SHELLEY. Capt.
                             Adjt. 2/5th North Staffs Regt.

Issued at 3.15 p.m.

Distribution - Normal.

APPENDIX 3

SECRET.   BATTALION OPERATION ORDERS No. 44.   Copy No. 8.
                          - by -   (War Diary).
                  LIEUT-COL. H. JOHNSON,
                        Commanding   In the Field,
               2/5th Bn. NORTH STAFFORD REGIMENT.   25/9/17.

Ref. Maps Sheet 28 N.W. 1/20000.
     "   28 N.W. 2 and N.E.1. 1/10000.

---

1. The 176th Infantry Brigade has relieved the 165th Inf. Bde. and are relieving the 164th Inf. Bde. to-night.
   The 2/5th North Staffs Regt will be the Left Support Battalion, the 2/6th North Staffs Regt being in the Front Line on the Left.

2. Companies will be ready to move off in the order, H.Q., B, C, A, D, at 4.30 p.m. 100 Yards interval will be maintained between Platoons; transport and pack ponies will move off in front of their Companies. Route:- Railway Crossing, H.12.b.2.8., cross-roads I.1.c.1.5., Canal Crossing I.2.c.1.5., cross-roads I.2.d.1.7. thence through ST. JEAN and WIELTJE.

3. "B" and "C" Companies will take up a position in the neighbourhood of SPREE and POND Farms. "A" Coy will be in CALL RESERVE Trench and the Trenches in the rear and "D" Coy in CAMBRAI RESERVE Trench, support and CAMBRAI Trench.

4. One pick or shovel, in the proportion 4 shovels to 1 pick, will be drawn from the Brigade Dump at C.23.c.25.10, junction of WIELTJE-GRAVANTAFEL Road with old GERMAN FRONT LINE Trench as each Platoon passes this position; the R.S.M. will be there to issue the tools.

5. The unexpended portion of the day's ration and rations for one day will be carried.

6. All stretchers will be carried on the Maltese Cart and Company Stretcher-Bearers will collect their stretchers from the R.A.P. while the remainder are drawing tools. The Maltese Cart will follow in the rear of H.Q.

7. Transport Arrangements.

   "B" and   8 Pack Ponies, 4 per Coy for L.G. Magazines (i.e. 30
   "C" Coys.   magazines and spare parts bag to be carried on each
                  pony).
                  8 Pack Ponies, 4 per Coy for water (i.e. 24 tins per
                  Coy, 6 per pony).
                  2 Pack Ponies, 1 per Coy, for Mess stores.

   "A" and   2 G.S. Limbers, 1 per Coy to carry L.G. Magazines, spare
   "D" Coys.   parts bag, water and mess stores, 22 tins of water per
                  Company.

   H.Q.   Maltese Cart, for M.O's. Stores, Stretchers, H.Q. Mess
                  stores, and 8 tins of water.

8. Companies will report when in position, giving the position of their headquarters.

9. Position of Bn. H.Q. C.23.c.35.35.

10. The R.A.P. will be at C.23.c.3.7. or near to.

11. Unless otherwise ordered, transport with rations and water will arrive at junction of CALL TRENCH with WIELTJE-GRAVANTAFEL Road at 5.30 p.m. daily. Companies will send guides to this point to direct.

12. Acknowledge.

                                      (Sd) V. B. SHELLEY. Capt.
                                      Adjt. 2/5th North Stafford Regt.
Issued at 3 p.m.
   Copies to:- 1. File.   5. "C" Coy.
               2. Major Bladen.   6. "D" Coy.
               3. "A" Coy.   7. M.O.
               4. "B" "   8. War Diary.

APPENDIX --- 4

Copy No. 8.
(War Diary).

SECRET.   Amendments to Bn. Operation
           Orders No. 44.
           ----

1. Reference para. 2 — Companies will be ready to move off at 5.30 p.m. Box Respirators will be worn in the "Alert" position.

2. Reference para. 3. — Dispositions will be as under:—

   "C" Coy.   2 Platoons.   DONT TRENCH.
               1   "   West to WIELTJE Road
                              D.13.c.5.3. — C.18.d.8.6.

   "B" Coy.   1 Platoon.   FORT HILL.
                              C.18.b.2.5.
               1   "   C.18.b.8.8.
               1   "   C.18.b.8.6.

   "A" Coy.   CALL RESERVE Trench.

   "D" "   CAMBRAI Trench.

3. Guides will be met at Bde. H.Q. at 7 p.m.

4. Reference para. 8 — Bn. H.Q. will be at

                              CAPRICORN REDOUBT.
                                    C.18.d.4.5.

                              (Sd) V. B. SHELLEY.   Capt.
                              Adjt. 2/5th North Stafford Regt.

Issued at 5 p.m.

Copies as for Bn. Operation Orders No. 44.

APPENDIX - 5

SECRET.   BATTALION OPERATION ORDERS No. 47,   (Copy for War Diary).
- by -
LIEUT.COL. H. JOHNSON,
Commanding   In the Field,
2/5th Bn. NORTH STAFFORD REGIMENT.   25/9/17.

Ref. Sheet 28.N.W. & N.E. 1/10000.

---

1. The 59th Division will attack on Zero Day. The 177th Bde. will attack on the right, and the 178th Brigade will attack on the left. The 175th Bde., 58th Division, will attack on the left of the 178th Bde. The 2/5th North Staff's Regt will be in reserve to 178th Bde.

2. The right boundary of 178th Bde. is a line from GALLIPOLI, D.13.d.5.1. - GALLIPOLI COPSE, D.14.c.5.2. - OTTO FARM, D.15.a.2.0. The left boundary of the 178th Bde. is the line of the HANEBEEK and thence along D.8.d.0.0. - D.9.c.0.0.
   The dividing lines between Battalions of the 178th Bde. is the WIELTJE ROAD.

3. The 2/5th North Stafford Regt will assemble in CAPRICORN Trenches, C.18.c.
   "A" Coy and "D" Coy will be in the FRONT Line.
   "B" "   and "C" "   will be in the SUPPORT Line.

   "A" and "B" Coys on the left of the WIELTJE ROAD.
   "C" and "D" Coys on the right "   "   "

   "B" and "C" Coys will be 100 yds in the rear of CAPRICORN Trench.
   Bn. H.Q. and R.A.P. will be at the PILLBOX, 50 yds in front of "A" Coy.
   After the Bn. is in position Company Commanders will assemble at Bn. H.Q. for further orders.

4. Dress and Equipment.
   As for yesterday's operations. Each man will move from present Billets fully equipped.

5. RATIONS.
   Emergency rations and one day's rations, with a Haversack Ration, will be carried. Separate arrangements are being made for the Haversack Ration.
   The greatest economy must be exercised by all ranks in the consumption of water as it may be difficult to get supplies.

6. No Transport will accompany the Battalion.

7. Throughout operations, unless other orders are issued, the R.A.P. will be near Bn. H.Q. The 16 Stretcher Bearers, without rifles, will act under orders of M.O. (and will report to him before leaving Billets) - to bring in casualties. The reserve 4 Stretcher Bearers per Company will carry rifles and 50 rounds S.A.A. and proceed with their Companies to render First Aid.

8. Companies will move off at the following times:-
   "D" Coy.   12 midnight.
   "A" "   12.15 a.m.
   "C" "   12.30 a.m.
   "B" "   12.45 a.m.
   Headquarters will be with the leading Platoon of "D" Coy.
   Starting Point - the Water Tower, YPRES - 2 minutes interval between Platoons.

9. SUPPLIES.
   Pack Animals, with supplies for Thursday, will be at SPREE FARM at 6 p.m. Companies will send Ration Parties at above time to meet same, and guide Pack Ponies as far forward as possible before unloading.

10. AEROPLANES.
    Only the most advanced Infantry will light Red Flares, or signal with the Watson Fans to the Aeroplanes when called upon.
    Contact aeroplanes will have the usual markings.
    Counter-attack aeroplanes will fly continuously throughout the day from

(Contd).

ZERO till DUSK. They will draw the attention of attacking Infantry to any sign of counter-attack developing as follows:-
(a) One long blast on KLAXON horn.
(b) Smoke bomb will be discharged. This bomb bursts about 100 feet below the machine into a white parachute flare, which leaves a long trail of brown smoke about a foot broad. Too much reliance must not be placed upon the smoke bombs, as the numbers are limited.

11. The Battalion will remain in CAPRICORN Trenches until orders are received to move forward, when they will tape up a position about the "LAN" of LANGEMARCK, square 14.c.

                                        (Sd) V. B. SHELLEY. Capt.
                                  Adjt. 2/5th North Stafford Regt.

Issued at 6 p.m.

Copies to:-
    1 File.
    2. "A" Coy.
    3. "B" "
    4. "C" "
    5. "D" "
    6. M.O.

Army Form C. 2118.

WAR DIARY
or
INTELLIGENCE SUMMARY
(Erase heading not required.)

Vol 9

Confidential

Original War Diary
of
2/5 North Staffs Regiment

From 1st Oct 1917
To 31st Oct 1917

Army Form C. 2118.

WAR DIARY
or
INTELLIGENCE SUMMARY

(Erase heading not required.)

Volume 2. October 1917

Instructions regarding War Diaries and Intelligence Summaries are contained in F. S. Regs., Part II. and the Staff Manual respectively. Title Pages will be prepared in manuscript.

Page 46

Place	Date	Hour	Summary of Events and Information	Remarks and references to Appendices
WATOU	1st		Strength 37 Officers 828 other ranks, includes 1 Officer & 9 ORs reinforcements at 59th Div Reinforcement Depot, ST OMER. The 59th Div had Artillery & three Field Companies moved to the STEENBECQUE area. The 2/5th North Stafford Regt moving off at 7.0 a.m. in motor lorries to CURRBECQUE via HAZEBROUCK STEENBECQUE, and HIRE arriving at destination at 1-30 p.m. the Battalion being billeted, the transport moved off at 5-30 a.m. by road and arrived at CURRBECQUE at 7.0 p.m.	Reference Map Sheet N.27 & 3ROK. S.M. 1/100,000 (a) (a) (a) (a) (a) (a)
CURRBECQUE	2nd		In Army Reserve. Inspections and cleaning up, in the afternoon the Brigade to deem of the G.O.C. 59th Division.	
"	3rd		Inspections & interior economy	
"	4th		Bath Parade. Church Parade, Thanksgiving and Platoon training	
"	5th	1.0 a.m.	Reinforcement from 59th Depot Battn arrived :- 3 Officers; Capt. T.H. Hogg, 11th N. Staff. Regt, Capt. T.C. Gevers, 1/6th N. Staff. Regt & 2/Lieut. M.P. Shed and 205 other ranks.	
"	6th		Company & Platoon training. Vet, Lectures and interior economy	
"	7th	8.0 a.m.	The Battn moved to CREPY marching about two thirds of the distance and completing the move by motor Bus, arriving at destination about 2 p.m. The Battn was billeted in Barns.	

WAR DIARY
INTELLIGENCE SUMMARY

Army Form C. 2118.

VOLUME 2 - OCTOBER 1917

PAGE 47

Place	Date	Hour	Summary of Events and Information	Remarks and references to Appendices
CRÉPY	8th		In Army Reserve. Battalion and Company Training	Ita
	9th		"	Ita
	10th	7 am	Battalion moved to HERSIN by motor bus and then marched to SAINS-EN-GOHELLE, Fosse 10, arriving about 3 pm.	Ita
SAINS-EN-GOHELLE	11th		Interior Economy	Ita Ref. Map LENS 1/10,000
	12th	9.30 am	In Divisional Reserve. Battalion moved by Route March to NOULETTE HUTS via BOYEFFLES to relieve the Reserve Canadian Battalion of the 1st Canadian Division. The Brass took over the Quartermasters Stores at BOUVIGNY - BOYEFFLES from the 4th Canadian Battalion.	Ita
NOULETTE HUTS	13th	6.30 pm	In Brigade Reserve. Wet morning, no parades. At 6.30 pm the Battn moved up to relieve the 4th Canadian Battn of the 1st Canadian Brigade who were holding a front extending from N 20 a 30 45 to N 13 d 70 95 this front consisted of a series of advanced posts in trenches (known as the GREEN LINE) in the rear and supports in front. 1 Coy in support ARGYLE, AMALGAM and ALOOF trenches, ACONITE and AMULET in the rear and supports in front, 1 in support. This area is held by 2 Companies in front. Relief was reported complete at 1.15 am.	Ref LENS 1/10,000 36 c. SW.I Ita
LIÉVIN and LENS	14th		The disposition of the Battn is as follows:- B Company held the left front extending from N 13.6.60 to N 13 d 9.1. C Co. held the right front extending from N 13 d 9.1 to N 24 d 00.46. B Co. HQ at N 13 c 9 b. C/Co HQ N 20 a 0.6. A company in support (CRONY CROOK) & platoon at central units. Company HQ at M 17 d 8.2 N 19. B Company in support at M 23 d 2.7 Battn O.P M 24 a 30.70 D Company in right support at M 23.b.3.0 and Coy HQ at M 23 d.	Ita

Army Form C. 2118.

WAR DIARY
or
INTELLIGENCE SUMMARY
(Erase heading not required.)

PAGE 48   VOLUME 2 - OCTOBER 1917

Place	Date	Hour	Summary of Events and Information	Remarks and references to Appendices
LIEVIN and LENS	15th 16th		Battalion holding the line in Brigade left front sector.	Ref: LENS 36 c. S.W.1 1/10,000
	17th	8.0	Inter Company relief took place, commencing at dusk. "A" Company relieving "B" Company in the left front line - "D" Company relieving "C" Company in the right front line - On completion of relief B & C Companies took up positions as support and reserve Companies respectively. "B" Company in support in cellars annexes to N.19 a 6.5. with Coy H.Q at N.19 a 42.43 "C" Company in reserve in cellars entrances 2 platoons about M.23 6 60.03. G. M.23.6 90.09. and 1 platoon about M.23 6 45.00. Coy H.Q at M.23.d 82.93. Relief was reported complete at 3 am 18th/10/17 Battalion holding the line in Brigade left front sector.	Insta Insta Insta Insta
	18th to 19th	8.0 8.0		
	20th 21st		Commencing at dusk this evening the Battalion was relieved by the 2/6 North Staffs Regt returning to LIEVIN as support Battalion on completion of relief at 11.15 pm. During this tour of duty in the line.	Insta

Total Casualties during this tour of duty in the line.

	KILLED	WOUNDED	SELF INFLICTED WOUNDS	MISSING
OFFICERS	Nil	Nil	Nil	Nil
O.R.'s	12	24	4	1

Army Form C. 2118.

WAR DIARY
or
INTELLIGENCE SUMMARY
(Erase heading not required.)

PAGE 40.   VOLUME 2 - OCTOBER 1917.

Place	Date	Hour	Summary of Events and Information	Remarks and references to Appendices
LIEVIN	22nd		Battalion in Brigade Support - disposition as follows:- Battn H.Q. M23.c.3.3 "A" Coy M22.d.9.1 "B" Coy M22.d.6.5.1.5 "D" Coy M28.c.50.6.3 R.A.P M23.c.2.4 "C" Coy M22.d.8.5.9.5	Ref LENS 36c SW 1 1/10,000
	23rd		Companies employed working in BLUE LINE at night.	Ditto
	24th		Battalion in Brigade Support. All available men were employed working in the BLUE LINE at night.	Ditto
	25th		Do	Ditto
			Battalion in Brigade Support. No working parties found for BLUE LINE on account of approach for protection against the enemy.	Ditto
	26th		Battalion in Brigade Support. Work in BLUE LINE	Ditto
	27th		Do	Ditto
	28th		Do	
	29th		The 178th Inf Bde in the LENS Sector to relieved by the 174th Inf Bde. The 2/5 B Staff Regt being relieved by the 2/4 Lincoln Regt. relief being reported complete at 10-0 p.m. The Battalion entrained from REDMILL SIDING (M27.d.7.9) - proceeding by Light Railway to GOUY - SERVINS - where the Battalion is billeted in Brateau and hub refugees. Move complete at 2.15 p.m. on the 30th inst.	108
GOUY-SERVINS	30"		In Divisional Reserve. Parades for various economy and cleaning.	108
"	31st		Ditto. Inspection of Battalion by C.O., Bathing etc.	108

Gary Johnson Lieut-Col.
Cmdg. 2/5 N. Stafford Regt.
31-10-17

Army Form C. 2118.

WAR DIARY
or
INTELLIGENCE SUMMARY.
(Erase heading not required.)

Vol 10

Original
War Diary
of
75th North Staffs Regiment
from 1st May 17
to 30th June 1917

Place	Date	Hour	Summary of Events and Information	Remarks and references to Appendices

Instructions regarding War Diaries and Intelligence Summaries are contained in F. S. Regs., Part II. and the Staff Manual respectively. Title pages will be prepared in manuscript.

WAR DIARY or INTELLIGENCE SUMMARY

Army Form C. 2118.

2/5th B. Staffs Regt.

VOLUME 2. NOVEMBER 1917

Page 50

Place	Date	Hour	Summary of Events and Information	Remarks and references to Appendices
GOUY--SERVINS	1st		In Divisional Reserve. Training, in the afternoon the Battalion attended a Brigade Parade for the presentation of medals & cards for services during the recent operations nr Cithen, the undermentioned N.C.Os men received:- Divisional Cards:- 40278 A/Sgt Bourne K.R. 16614 Pte Green F.W. / 200561 Sgt Gougne T. 200763 " Parkes J. / 202189 Pte Carlton F.R. 202334 " Pidgen A. / 202333 " Jones F. 40158 " Rhodes T. / 300142 Sgt Hammack M. 300453 " Ridgway F. / 202141 " Hoyle H. 11075 " Blew R. / 200178 " Kent F. 201905 " Marshall J.	W.D.
"	2nd		Company & Platoon Training	Air
"	3rd		Ditto.	Air
"	4th		Company & Platoon Training	Air
"	5th		Battalion Church Parade.	
"	6th		Range. All Companies. In the afternoon the Transport was inspected by the Divisional General. Parade for Interior Economy & Cleaning. At 5:30pm the Battalion entrained from GOUY SERVINS STN. (N.5.a.4.2.) three-quarters by Light Railway Sheet 36 b/c to RED TRENCH (S.12.a.2.9.) for the purpose of relieving the Vim 1/40000 2/8th Sherwood Foresters who were holding a front extending from SW 3 1/20000 N 33. a. 0.4. on the right to SOUCHEZ RIVER on the left. Quebec	Air

WAR DIARY or INTELLIGENCE SUMMARY

Army Form C. 2118.

VOLUME 2 November 1917.

Place	Date	Hour	Summary of Events and Information	Remarks and references to Appendices
GOVT. SEVINS.	6th.		This front is divided into 2 Subsectors the right subsector from the right boundary to the point N.26.d.80.25, the left subsector from N.26.d.15.40 to the left boundary. The 2 subsectors are separated by floods. Relief was reported complete at 1.30 a.m.	Ahn.
LA COULOTTE	7th.		The disposition of the Battalion is as follows. Batt H.Q. Brewery LA COULOTTE N.31.c.5.1. R.A.P. N.31.c.5.1. B. Company held the left front consisting of ELEV. and ELEY SUPPORT TRENCHES, with advanced Post One Platoon in Support on SASKATOON Rd at N.31.c.18.26, & one Platoon in Reserve at B.H.Q. N.31.c.5.1. Company H.Q. at N.26.c.15.30. C. Coy. held the right front in AVION with D¹ PIXIE TARLING as their front line trench with advanced posts. Half Platoon in Support at N.32.b.75.75. Gnl Platoon in Reserve at N.32.c.3.1. C. Coy. H.Q. at N.32.d.62.90. D. Coy. in Support in AVION TRENCH. with H.Q. at N.32.d.35.50. A. Coy in Reserve at B.H.Q with H.Q. at N.31.c.5.1.	Ref Sheet 36 B + C 1/20000 M.M.Y. 36.C. S.W.3 1/10000 QUEBEC R¹ 1/10000
"	8th		Battalion holding the line in Brigade left front Sector.	
"	9th		" " " " " " "	
"	10th		After Company Relief took place after dusk "D" Company relieving "C" Coy. in the front line on the right, & "A" Coy relieving "B" Coy in the front line on the left. On completion of relief "C" & "B" Coy's became Support & reserve Coy's respectively. A. Coy H.Q. at N.26.c.15.30. B. Coy H.Q. at N.31.c.5.1. C. Coy H.Q at N.32.d.35.50. D. Coy H.Q. at N.32.d.62.90. Relief was reported complete at 10.30 p.m. 11/11/17.	Ahn.
"	11th		Battalion holding the line in Brigade left front Sector	Ahn.

WAR DIARY or INTELLIGENCE SUMMARY

Army Form C. 2118.

Page 52 VOLUME 2   November 1917

Place	Date	Hour	Summary of Events and Information	Remarks and references to Appendices
LA COULOTTE	12th 13th		Battalion holding the line in Brigade Left Front Sector. Commanding officer dusk the Battalion was relieved by the 2/6th North Staffs Regt. returning to the RED TRENCH AREA as Left Support Battalion on completion of relief. Casualties during this tour of duty in the line: Killed Wounded Self Inflicted Missing Wounded (Gas Shell) OFFICERS Nil Nil Nil Nil Nil O.R's Nil 7 2 Nil 47	Sheet 36 B/C 1/40000 Sheet 36c SW3 1/20000 Quebec Rd 1/10000
RED TRENCH	14th		Battalion in Brigade Support. Dispositions as follows:- Battalion Hq S.6.b.1.0. "A" Coy Hq S.5.b.48.88. "B" Coy Hq S.6.c.09.82 "C" Coy Hq S.12.a.19.92. "D" Coy Hq S.6.d.03.93. Companies employed on day's work working & carrying parties.	
"	15th		Battalion in Brigade Support. Battalion employed on working & carrying parties.	
"	16th		The 16th Infantry Bde on the AVION Sector is relieved by the 3rd Canadian Infantry Bde. The 2/5th North Staffs Regt is relieved by the 15th Canadian Battalion. The relief being reported complete by 7 p.m. when the battalion proceeded to SOUCHEZ CAMP, arriving about 1 a.m. the 17th/11/19 17. Move complete by 2.0 a.m. 17/11/1917.	
SOUCHEZ CAMP	17th		The Battalion moved by Route March to GOUY SERVINS.	
GOUY SERVINS	18th		In Divisional Reserve. The Battalion moved to PETIT SERVINS.	
PETIT SERVINS	19th		The Division is transferred from the 1st Corps 1st Army to the V Corps, 3rd Army & is moved by Route March to BERNEVILLE via ACQ, HAUTE-AVESNE	Sheet 36b 1/40000 Sheet 51b 1/10000

WAR DIARY
or
INTELLIGENCE SUMMARY
(Erase heading not required.)

Army Form C. 2118.

VOLUME 2   November 1917

Place	Date	Hour	Summary of Events and Information	Remarks and references to Appendices
BERNYVILLE	20th		and AGNEZ-LES-DUISANS arriving at 6 pm when the Battalion received orders to move at 1½ hours notice. In Army Reserve.	Sheet 31B & 51C 1/40,000 LENS 11 1/100,000
"	21st		Parades for Infantry Economy & Cleaning.	Ah
			Wd. Lectures & Interior Economy. At 11.30 pm the Battalion is moved by Route March to COURCELLES LE COMTE arriving about 4.30 am on the 22nd/11/1917.	Sheet 51C Arras 1/40,000
COURCELLES LE COMTE	22nd		No Parades. Cleaning	Ah
"	23rd		Company & Platoon Training. The Battalion is moved by Route March to the Railway Stn BIHUCOURT WEST 9.16 & 9.9. where it is entrained for FINS & is again moved by Route March to HEUDICOURT arriving about 9.30 pm	Ah
HEUDICOURT	24th		In Corps Reserve. Parades for Interior Economy & Cleaning. The Division is transferred from the V.Corps Third Army to the III Corps III Army	Ah
"	25th		Church Services & Interior Economy	Ah
"	26th		Company & Platoon training. In the afternoon 3 Infantry Schemes no Beyond out to by all officers by the Brigadier.	Ah
"	27th		Company & Platoon training. At 11.30 am the Battalion is ordered to move forward & relieve the 2nd Grenadier Guards in reserve Ruedge, S.W. of RIBECOURT. The Battalion is moved by Route March at 12.30 pm & arrives about 5 pm. At 12.0 clock midnight 16 Officers & 2 Company pre Content go forward to reconnoitre the ground & line held by the 1st Batt Coldstream Guards.	Ah 51C Army 20,000 MASNIERES 20,000 NURLU 20,000 WIERGES 20,000

Page 53

WAR DIARY or INTELLIGENCE SUMMARY

Page 54 VOLUME 2 November 1917

Place	Date	Hour	Summary of Events and Information	Remarks and references to Appendices
RIBECOURT	28th		In Reserve to the Guards Division. The Disposition of the Battalion is as follows. B.H.Q. in RIBECOURT at L.25.c.6.9. A, B, C, & D Coys. in reserve trenches in the "HINDENBURG LINE" S.W. of RIBECOURT running through K36.a & K36.c. At 5.30 pm the 1/6th Bn. was ordered to move forward to relieve the 2nd Guards Bde. in the FONTAINE NOTRE DAME Sector. The 2/5th North Staffs Regt. relieving the 1st Batt Grenadier Guards, the Centre Front Battalion. Completion of relief was reported at 9.45 pm.	SHEET 57C 1/40000 MOEUVRES 1/20000 NIERGNES 1/20000 O.W.
SOUTH OF BOURLON WOOD	29th		This front extended from F.21.c.3.7. exclusive to F.14.d.1.6. & onwards a series of detached posts, held by three Companies. B Company on the left with Coy HQrs at F.14.D.2.3. C Coy Centre with HQrs at F.14.d.2.3. & D Coy on the right with HQrs at F.21.d.4.4. A Coy in Support with HQ at F.20.c.33.10. Batt HQ at F.20.c.82.17. R.A.P at F.20.c.82.17. After dusk 3 Platoons of D Coy with HQrs were withdrawn from the front line to the Support line and had their HQ at F.21.b.20.42. Rations were taken direct to Coys in their posns. A Coy & D Coys (less 1 platoon) were employed on trenching & carrying parties at night.	SHEET 57C 1/40000 MOEUVRES 1/20000 NIERGNES 1/20000 O.W.
" "	30th		Battalion holding the line. In the Brigade Centre. Between 11 + 12 o'clock am the 2/5 North Staffs were responsible for beating off a very heavy enemy counter attack. Good work was carried out by the front Coy Commanders who inflicted severe casualties on the	

Army Form C. 2118.

WAR DIARY
or
INTELLIGENCE SUMMARY
(Erase heading not required.)

VOLUME 2 November 1917

Place	Date	Hour	Summary of Events and Information	Remarks and references to Appendices
S.of BOURLON WOOD	30th	enemy	Good work was also carried out by Cpl Thomas of "C" Coy by reconnoitring the southern edge of copse at F.21.a.36.85. & Factory at F.15a.38.05. in broad daylight & in full view of the enemy. Useful information was obtained & good sniping was done. The total number of casualties sustained during the attack were:- Officers killed 1, wounded 5, missing nil O.R. 16 36 (Signed) W. Murray Lieut. Col. Comdg 2/5th North Staffs	59.C. 40000 MOEUVRES 20000 MIERGNES 20000 AUBIGNY 20000

Army Form C. 2118.

WAR DIARY
or
INTELLIGENCE SUMMARY.
(Erase heading not required.)

Confidential

Original

War Diary
of
2½th North Staffs Regiment

From 1st Dec 1914.
To 31st Dec 1914.

WAR DIARY or INTELLIGENCE SUMMARY

Army Form C. 2118.

Page 56   VOLUME 2   DECEMBER 1917.

Place	Date	Hour	Summary of Events and Information	Remarks and references to Appendices
South of BOURLON WOOD	1st		The Battalion holding the line in the Brigade Centre. At 12.30 p.m. the right hand Company were responsible for breaking up another counter attack by the enemy on the right brigade front & inflicting between 90 & 105 casualties on the enemy by rifle & Lewis gun fire. During this operation the 2/5th Notts Staffs suffered one casualty.	57 C/4 WOOD MOEUVRES 1/10000 NIERGNES 1/20000 Oln.
"	2nd		The Battalion holding the line in the Brigade Centre. The 1/4th Lnd Bde. so relieved by the 197th Inf. Bde. The 2/5th Notts Staffs is relieved by the 2/5th Lincolns. The relief being reported complete by 10 p.m. when the Battalion proceeded to the HINDENBURG SUPPORT LINE at Louverin	57 C. N.E. 1/20000 Oln.
PLESQUIERES	3rd		The disposition of the Battalion is as follows: A & B Coys in trenches from K23 & 5. to junction of FLESQUIERES-HAVRINCOURT ROAD K23 & 3.5. D Coys on the right B Coy on the Left. Bn HQ at K24.a.10.55 C Coys on either side of B HQ are at the disposal of G.O.C. 197th Inf Bde. All Coys on working parties at night.	Oln.
"	4th		The Battalion in the HINDENBURG Support line. Battalion on working parties digging deliveries for the village of FLESQUIERES.	57 C/N ½ 1/20000 Oln
"	5th		About 2 a.m. the 2/5th Notts Staffs went relieved by the 1/8th Lincoln Regt the relief being reported complete by 3.45 a.m. when the Battalion proceeded the METZE by route march via K23.B. Central thence S.W. through K23.C.9.2. K19.B. & Q.H.d. crossroads K29 & 1. K27.2.1.9. thence South through K35.a. Q.H.d. to the crossroads at Q.10.b.9.6. thence Q.20.b.05. to Q.20.a.5.5. At 12 noon the Battalion moved by Route March to PIONEER CAMP S.W. of YPRES P.25.c.5.5 during this tour in the line the 2/5th North Staffs Regt captured	Oln.

2449 Wt. W14957/M90 750.000 1/16 J.B.C. & A. Forms/C.2118/12.

WAR DIARY or INTELLIGENCE SUMMARY

Army Form C. 2118.

(Erase heading not required.)

VOLUME 2. December 1917.

Place	Date	Hour	Summary of Events and Information	Remarks and references to Appendices
	5th		2 German Machine Guns. Total Casualties during this tour of duty in the line. Killed Wounded Self Inflicted Missing Accidentally Wounded	SY/C/40000
			OFFICERS 1 Nil Nil Nil	
			O.R's 16 5 1 1	Ch
PIONEER CAMP.	6th		In Divisional Reserve. Company + Platoon training + Parades for Soldiers Economy	Ch.
"	7th		Company + Platoon training. Bathing Parades	Ch.
"	8th		Company + Platoon training. Bathing Parades.	Ch.
"	9th		Battn Parade. Church Parade. Thanksgiving + Bathing Parades	Ch.
			A Composite Brigade is formed + is composed of 3 Battalions of the 178th Inf. Bde + the 2/5th Yorks Staffs + 2/5th South Staffs Regts under Lt Colonel Stansfield D.S.O. Commandant of 178 Composite Brigade. Orders are received that the Composite Brigade will relieve the 177th and 176th Bdes on the	576 H.E. MISSING
			FLESQUIRES Sector on the nights 9/10th, 10/11th, + 11/12 December. The 2/5 Yorks Staffs to relieve the 2/4th Lincolns Regt on the night of the 10th Dec. on the right Sector of the HINDENBURG SUPPORT trench from K 24 a. 8.8. to K 19 a. 9.3.	SY/G/40000
	10th		At 12 noon the Battalion marched by route March to the HINDENBURG SUPPORT via METZ + TRESCAULT for the purpose of relieving the 2/4th Lincolns Regt on the right Brigade Support. The relief being reported complete at 8 pm. The Battalion to enthusiast in carrying parties.	Ch.
HINDENBURG SUPPORT	11th		The Battalion in the HINDENBURG SUPPORT LINE. One platoon of the Rocket of the	Ch.

WAR DIARY or INTELLIGENCE SUMMARY

Army Form C. 2118

(Erase heading not required.)

Volume 2. December 1917. Page 58.

Place	Date	Hour	Summary of Events and Information	Remarks and references to Appendices
	11th		is as follows Battalion Headquarters K24.a.7.3. R.A.P. K24.a.8.5. A.Coy Hqtrs K24.a.6.3. B.Coy Hqtrs K24.b.4.6. C.Coy Hqtrs K24.b.4.1. D.Coy Hqtrs K24.b.6.6. B.Coy employed on working parties by R.E's. A.C. D.Coys. General working parties.	59 C.N.E. MARCOING 57c Cen
HINDENBURG SUPPORT	12th		In support to the 2/8th Sherwood Foresters who are holding the front line in the right FLESQUIERES Sector. Battalion employed on working & carrying parties	On
"	13th		Into Battalion relief took place the 2/5th Sherwood Foresters relieving the 2/8th Sherwood Foresters on the right front FLESQUIERES Sector	On
FLESQUIERES	14th		The Battalion holding the line in the right FLESQUIERES Sector. The dispositions of the Battalion is as follows, D.Coy holding the right front trenches at L13.c.12.36, with C.Coy in Support Hqtrs at L9.a.0.5.0. Sect 5.7C A.Coy holding the left front trenches at K18.b.30.55 with B.Coy in Support. Hqtrs at K18.a.80.15. At 9.20 p.m. two platoons of D.Coy under the Command of 2/Lt Gard & 2/Lt Belsky left the British front line to take up a position for the purpose of examining the enemy trenches at L13.a.5.7. Q at 11 p.m. after much firing they moved forward & entered the enemy trenches which were unoccupied. The enemy, by the light from the Vital Casualties 10th Killed & 5 wounded 2/Lt Belsky severely wounded	NERGNES 20000 Seets 57C New 100000 On

1875 Wt. W593/826 1,000,000 4/15 J.B.C. & A. A.D.S.S./Forms/C. 2118.

Army Form C. 2118.

WAR DIARY
or
INTELLIGENCE SUMMARY

(Erase heading not required.)

Instructions regarding War Diaries and Intelligence Summaries are contained in F. S. Regs., Part II. and the Staff Manual respectively. Title Pages will be prepared in manuscript.

VOLUME 2 December 1917.

Place	Date	Hour	Summary of Events and Information	Remarks and references to Appendices
FLESQUIERES	15th		The Battalion holding the line in the right FLESQUIERES SECTOR. The Battalion entrenched at nights on defining, digging & carrying parties. A & D Companies each sending up a returna working patrol. Enemy enemy movements at R.18.b.	
"	16th		The Battalion holding the line in the right FLESQUIERES SECTOR. A & D Coys Patrolling digging & carrying parties at nights.	
"	17th		The Battalion holding the line in the right FLESQUIERES SECTOR. Orders are received that the Coldstream Bde will be relieved by the 177th Inf Bde on the nights of 17/18th & 18/19th December. The 2/5th North Staff Regt will be relieved by the 2/4th Leicesters on the night of 18/19th.	
"	18th		Commencing at dusk the 2/5th North Staffs is relieved by the 2/4th Leicesters, relief being completed by 7.30 pm. The Battalion is then relieved by Ambulance march to the old British front line at TRESCAULT Q.4.a. & C. via RIBECOURT. Total Casualties during this tour of duty in the line.	
			OFFICERS Nil. Killed Wounded L.Belcher (Shocked) at Duty Nil.	
			OR's 3. 24. 3.	
TRESCAULT	19th		The Battalion in reserve trenches in the Old British front line at TRESCAULT. Working through Q.4.a. & C. with Battalion H.Q. at Q.4.c.55.60. General clean up. Orders are received that the 59th Division will be relieved from the 20th inst by the 19th Division.	
"	20th		The Coldstream Brigade is relieved by the 51st Inf Bde, the 2/5th North Staff Regt	

WAR DIARY
or
INTELLIGENCE SUMMARY
(Erase heading not required.)

Army Form C. 2118.

VOLUME 2   December 1917

Place	Date	Hour	Summary of Events and Information	Remarks and references to Appendices
BARASTRE	21st		Being relieved by the 9th Lincolns Regt. On completion of relief the 2/5th North Staffs moved by route march to BARASTRE via METZ, NEUVILLE VITASSE & BUS. On arrival at BARASTRE the 2/5th North St. Staffs + 2/5th South Staffs Regt. & the 172nd Machine Gun Coy came under the command of Lt. Col. H. Johnston. T.D.	Sheet 57C 1/40000 Am
"	22nd		In Army Reserve. Parade for Interior Economy & Inspection	Am
"	"		Parade for Interior Economy, Inspection & Bathing. Afternoon Inter-Platoon Football Matches. 7th Corp Commander saw Battn. Football Colours. Pte. 200561 Sgt Bygone J. Bey & 202535. Pte Joggood J." awarded the Military Medal to for Gallantry in Action during the enemy counter attack of Fontaine on Nov 30th 1917. The Divisional Commander has awarded Cards of Commendation to 202372 Pte Ashridge J. "C" Coy. for gallantry during 201389 " Slaw G.E. " the enemy counter attack on Nov. 30. 6. 1917. Battalion Church Parade	Am Am Am
	23rd			
	24th		Inspection at 10 a.m. by Company Commanders. Orders are received that the 59th Division will move to the LECOUROY area on the 2nd & 25th December 19.4.6. the 2/5 North Staffs will move to LIENCOURT on the 25th.	Sheet 57 C 1/40000 LENS II 1/100,000 Am
	25th		The Battalion moved by route march via VILLERS-au-FLOS, RIENCOURT-LES-BAPAUME to BAPAUME Station	Am

WAR DIARY
INTELLIGENCE SUMMARY

(Erase heading not required.)

Army Form C. 2118

Page 61. VOLUME 2. December 1917.

Place	Date	Hour	Summary of Events and Information	Remarks and references to Appendices
LIENCOURT	26th		Where it entrained for FREVENT Sin arrived at FREVENT the Battalion moved by route march to LIENCOURT arriving about 8 p.m.	Sheet 57C 1/40000
"	27th		In Army Reserve. General Cleaning up. Parades for Interior Economy.	App.
"	28th		Battalion Route March about 8 miles in the afternoon. Recreational Training. Company & Platoon Training.	App.
"	29th		Company & Platoon Training, Recreational Training, Inspection of Anti-Gas Appliances	App.
"	30th		Church Parades	App.
"	31st		Company Training. "C" Company range practices.	App.

The following copy of letters received from V Corps:—

(1) The Corps Commander hopes me to say that the patrolling carried out by the Division reports sent in reflect much credit on those concerned. He considers patrolling on the neight 15th Jeb especially good.

(2) 9 Bgd. B.G.E.S.
I Corps.

(2) On the withdrawal of the 59th Division from the line & on its departure from the V Corps, the Corps Commander wishes me to say how much appreciates the good work done by the Division during the time it has been under his Command. The Division has put up such good fighting qualities. Although not a fresh Division it would have been carried out both offensive & defensive duties & has been called upon to take the place of a Division of the Regular Army in the Corps. The Corps Commander will telegraph to General Ramsay in the Corps.

CW.

(3) 9 Bgd. B.G.E.S. V. Corps.

Gary Moore
Lieut. Col.
Comdg. 2/5 North Stafford Regt.

Army Form C. 2118.

WAR DIARY
or
INTELLIGENCE SUMMARY.
(Erase heading not required.)

59/176 Vol 12

Original

Confidential

War Diary
of
1/5th Bn. North Staffs Regiment

Jan 1st 1918 to 31st Jan 1918

Page 62.

Volume N2.

WAR DIARY
INTELLIGENCE SUMMARY

2/5th Bn. R. Staff Regt.

Army Form C. 2118

January 1918

Place	Date	Hour	Summary of Events and Information	Remarks and references to Appendices
LIENCOURT	1st		In G.H.Q Reserve. Company & Platoon Training. (III Corps, Third Army) The Bn. received the following Awards for Services during the recent operations during the CAMBRAI OFFENSIVE. Capt. T.E. Tebbetts ... } Military Cross. ... W.N. Bladen ...} 201928 Pte. J. Tunstall ... "B" Coy ... Distinguished Conduct Medal 6960 Sergt. J. Gorry ... ... Military Medal " ... ... Distinguished Conduct Medal Sept. 1918. and the following Honours & Awards in the New Years Honours List 1918. Capt. E. Barhart ... Military Cross 202830 Pte. E. Chambers ... "B" Coy ... Distinguished Conduct Medal 2nd Lieut. W. Haygreaves ... N Style } Mentioned in Despatches 200566 C.S.M. W. Wood ... "A" Coy } 200567 Sgt. (A/CSM) C. Hall ... II } Strength of Battalion. 36 Officers 804 ORs. away from Bn. detached, on command, leave, in hospital but not evacuated etc. 15 Off. 143 ORs	LENS 11. 1/100000
"	2nd		Company Training, Close order drill etc. Musketry on range at I.25.B.	
"	3rd		Inspection by the G.O.C 176th Inf. Bde.	FRANCE. 51c 1/40000.

Page 63   Volume 2

WAR DIARY
INTELLIGENCE SUMMARY 2/5th Bn. R. Staff Regt.
(Erase heading not required.)

Army Form C. 2118

Place	Date	Hour	Summary of Events and Information	Remarks and references to Appendices
LIENCOURT	4th		In G.H.Q. Reserve. (VI Corps Third Army) Company Training, Musketry.	USR
"	5th		" Company Training, Musketry.	USR
"	6th		" Church Parades.	USR
"	7th		" Company + Individual Training, Musketry	USR
"	8th		" Bayonet Tactical Training with Troops, Lewis Gun Training	USR
"	9th		" Battalion Tactical Exercise, Individual Training	USR
"	10th		" Company + Individual Training, Musketry	USR
"	11th		" Brigade Tactical Exercise with Troops, Lewis Gun Training	USR
"	12th		" Bn. Drill, Final Assault Practice on Range	USR
"	13th		" Church Parades	USR
"			MILITARY CROSS for services during the recent operation, when in Command of a Raiding Party, East of FLESQUIERES, Lieut. R.B.C. Aked.	USR
"	14th		" Individual Training & Musketry.	USR
"	15th		" Individual Training, Company Bombing Attacks at VI Corps School	USR
"	16th		" Company + Individual Training, Musketry	USR
"	17th		" "	USR

Page 64 Volume L

Army Form C. 2118

WAR DIARY
or
INTELLIGENCE SUMMARY

2/5th Bn. R. Staff. Regt.

(Erase heading not required.)

Place	Date	Hour	Summary of Events and Information	Remarks and references to Appendices
LIENCOURT	18th		Company Drill, Musketry, Lewis Gun Training.	App
"	19th		Bn. Drill, Final Assault Practice on Ridge	App
"	20th		Church Parades	App
"	21st		Company Training Musketry	App
"	22nd		"	App
"	23rd		Inspection by G.O.C. 59th Division.	App
"	24th		Company Training + Individual Training	App
"	25th		Brigade Tactical Exercise.	App
"	28th		Bn. Drill, Final Assault - Practice on Ridge	App
"			Draft of 1 Officer + 42 ORs arrive from 59th Bn. Depot, Glasgow, 2nd Lieut.	App
CRADDOCK	27th			App
"			Church Parades.	App
"	28th		Specialist + Individual Training, Musketry.	App
"	29th		Specialist + Individual Training	App
"	30		Company Training	App
			176 Bde Orders. A Coy winning Coy in Bde. 79, 82, 90 home dest. within time limit.	
			Draft 10 Officers and 197 O.R. posted from 1/5 North Staffs Regt. after amalgamation with this Unit, which	

WAR DIARY
or
INTELLIGENCE SUMMARY
(Erase heading not required.)

Army Form C. 2118

Place	Date	Hour	Summary of Events and Information	Remarks and references to Appendices
LIENCOURT	30.1.18 (contd)	—	G.H.Q. Reserve (w/Corps III Army) now becomes 5th Battn. Nott & Staff Regt. 9 this day/the undermentioned Officers & 128 O.R. joined this day. The remainder will join later. Capt. F.E. Weager M.C. 2/Lt. L.C. Grier Lt. W.E. Coulisham M.C. — q.m. Humphrey	Ret. 2M.
"	31.1.18	—	Specialist & Individual Training. Musketry n. Strength Battalion 46 Officers 1039 O.R. — Away from Battalion, attached, on courses, leave, in hospital but not evacuated 17 Officers 175 O.R. Chay Silveran Lt. Col. Comdg. 5th Bn Nott Staff Regt.	

www.ingramcontent.com/pod-product-compliance
Lightning Source LLC
Chambersburg PA
CBHW081441160426
43193CB00013B/2352